This book belongs to

_____

_____

Christine Thompson-Wells
Author, Qualified Professional, Accredited Educator &
Independent Writer
BA Education, Dip of Teaching, MACEA

We support Diabetes Type One & Motor Neuron Disease. 10% of the net sales
will be divided equally between both charities.

Our Mission:

Every child and adult have value and is important to us; therefore, we strive through online education and book publishing, to bring life skill education to all children and all families.

For Education Packages

See our book websites: www.how2books.com.au and
www.fullpotentialtraining.com.au
or Contact:
admin@fullpotentialtraining.com.au

HORMONES WITH HATS

MEETING CURRICULUM OBJECTIVES – UNITED KINGDOM (UK)

Natural body changes for girls between School Years 7 to 9, ages 11 to 14 years.

(Health and Wellbeing, Relationships, and Living in the Wider World)

Relationships Education, Relationships and Sex Education (RSE) and Health Education.

'Effective RSE does not encourage early sexual experimentation. It should teach young people to understand human sexuality and to respect themselves and others. It enables young people to mature, build their confidence and self-esteem and understand the reasons for delaying sexual activity. Effective RSE also supports people, throughout life, to develop safe, fulfilling, and healthy sexual relationships, at the appropriate time.'[1]

CURRICULUM OBJECTIVES – AUSTRALIA

Incorporating and supporting Year 7-9, ages 11-14 years. Personal, Social and Community Health (ACPPS070 – ACPS076 - ACPPS071 - ACPPS072 - ACPPS073 – and other related areas of the Curriculum including: TLF-IDM021182 Scootle.edu.au).

For School and family packages, please see Pages 112 - 113 for further information.

---

[1] Relationships and Sex Education (RSE) (Secondary) - GOV.UK (www.gov.uk)
Extracted from 'statutory guidance Relationships Education, Relationships and Sex Education (RSE) and Health Education & Australia: https://www.scootle.edu.au

If you have purchased this book without its cover, it may be a stolen book.

Neither the publisher or the author is under any obligation to provide professional services in anyway, legal, health or in any form which is related to this book, its contents advice or otherwise.

The law and practices vary from country to country and state to state.

If legal or professional information is required, the purchaser, or the reader should seek the information privately and best suited to their particular needs, and circumstances.

This is not a medical book. It is a book developed by the publisher to open the conversation about how the human body changes when growing up.

The author and publisher specifically disclaim any liability that may be incurred from the information within this book.
All rights reserved. No part of this book, including the interior design, images, cover design, diagrams, or any intellectual property (IP), icons and photographs may be reproduced or transmitted in any form by any means (electronic, photocopying, recording or otherwise) without the prior permission of the publisher. ©

Copyright© 2022 MSI Australia

All rights reserved.

ISBN: 978-0-6451314-1-3

Published by How2Books
Under licence from MSI Ltd, Australia
Company Registration No: 96963518255
NSW, Australia

See our website: www.how2books.com.au
Or contact by email: sales@how2books.com.au
Covers and Copyright owned by MSI, Australia

MSI acknowledges the author and images, text and photographs used in this book.

Children's books

Will Jones Space Adventures & The Money Formula – Book
Will Jones Space Adventures & The Money Formula – The Play
Will Jones & The Money Formula – Educator's Resource Pack
Will Jones Space Adventures & the Zadrilian Queen – Book
Will Jones Space Adventures & The Zadrilian Queen – Play
Will Jones Space Adventures & The Zadrilian Queen – Educator's Resource Pack
There are many more Will Jones Books To Come Out
Dora Damper Makes Honey Damper Bread
Potato Pete Goes to Market
Changes Facing Rosie
Changes Facing Kian
Changes Facing Jai
Changes Facing Caitlin

Books For Adults

Devils In Our Food
Recipes Without Devil Additives
How To Reduce Stress – Find Your Positive Head Space
Making Cash Flow
Selling Made Easy
Know Your Destination 'Go' Learn To Drive Your Mind
The Golden Book Of Whispering Poems and many more books
Hormones, Puberty & Your Child
Please see our website

Disclaimer

This is not a medical book and should not be used as such. The contents have been developed through observational theory and research (observational psychology). Information is also drawn from scientific literature, web search and personal enquiry.

The diagrams are for information and to enhance the meaning of the written text. Statements, information, and ideas within this book are for education purposes only. The text presented allows the reader to draw their own conclusions on the content offered.

Always consult with your doctor for possible illness or underlying illness. Christine Thompson-Wells (MSI) Australia, How2Books.com.au and Full Potential Training.com.au, cannot be held liable for any errors or omissions.

PREFACE

The characters and story within this book are fictitious. If a similar name or identity is drawn from within the writing, it is purely coincidental. The stories are not representative of any one or more individuals. The stories come together through my own unique and individual teaching and life experiences that are brought together to create this book.

Because all children worldwide go through similar bodily changes at similar times growing up, the stories connect with different children worldwide. The places where children are living are used to ground the story. The locations are destinations I have visited on my own life journey.

Each book targets different age and growth spans, and the story base incorporates children's stories, taking into account, some artistic thought, and writing.

The four books (two for boys and two for girls) are within the series: 'Changes', Children Growing Up, have been designed in a narrative form: (story telling) to assist children and to allow them to naturally adapt to their environment while they go through the different child to adult stages.

It is with sensitivity, that I acknowledge different cultures and traditions, this, and to my best ability, is understood in the writing, illustrations, and storytelling.

HOW TO USE THIS BOOK

In a NEW and exciting approach, hormone characters help our children learn about how their body changes when growing up.

The chapters are the story book. This approach allows the young adult to come to grips with how their body and the way they think is changing.

Part Two introduces the adults to the story and the information the young person has learnt and how respect needs to work in all relationships.

Part Three allows both the young adult and older adults to work through the pages together. This process helps the family to celebrate the changes that all young people go through as they go into adulthood. By 'opening up' the conversation, young adults gain self-esteem, become ready for the changes their body is about to make, and become confident young people enjoying their journey into adulthood.

Part Four identifies the significance of how their brain, maturity and knowledge of the essential responsibilities that being a young adult brings into their life. By identifying, Involvement, Structure, Recall, Production, and Harvesting, then onto Consent, Friendship, Communication and Understanding, we are equipping our young adults with not only knowledge, but the social skills needed to confidently navigate into their future.

Part Five identifies how some hormones change the way the body reacts to different hormones; some hormones can lead to skin outbreaks and other skin irritations. This part helps the young adult to know how hygiene and care can, not only make them feel good, but add to their overall wellbeing.

Part Six is the journey that identifies how many young people have the desire to 'stretch their wings' and commit to different life challenges.

We encourage both boys and girls to read these books.

Christine

Contents   Page

Preface
How To Use This Book
Contents
'CHANGES' Children Face Difficult Times – From Child to Adult
Let's Re-cap
Introduction
CHAPTER ONE   1
The Birmingham Games 2022
CHAPTER TWO   11
A surprising interaction
CHAPTER THREE   20
Sheena takes the girls' home
CHAPTER FOUR   32
They all meet for afternoon tea
CHAPTER FIVE   39
Learning more about hormones
CHAPTER SIX   51
From a girl to a woman
PART TWO   71
Working Together – For Young Adults and Their Family
RESPECT
PART THREE   77
Working Together – For Young Adults and their Family
OPENING UP THE CONVERSATION –
CONTINUING THE JOURNEY
PART FOUR   90
Working Together – For Young Adults and their Family
INVOLVEMENT, STRUCTURE, RECALL, PRODUCTION and
HARVESTING – CONSENT, FRIENDSHIP, COMMUNICATION,
UNDERSTANDING YOUR GIRL, BUILDING HER SKILL
BASE AND WORKING WITH HER AMAZING BRAIN
PART FIVE   102
Working Together – For Young Adults and their Family
HYGEINE and CARE
PART SIX   109
Working Together – For Young Adults and their Family
A TIME OF LEARNING AND GROWTH
UNDERSTAND HOW THE HUMAN BODY GROWS and   113
MATURES
Online School Packages   114
Family Packages   115

'CHANGES'

CHILDREN FACE DIFFERENT SITUATIONS – FROM A CHILD TO AN ADULT

Facing the changes that the human body and brain go through are just some of the differences that all children go through as they go into adulthood.

Differences identified

Each stage of a child's life is similar but not the same, however, there are markers that will allow both young and older adults to identify different differences as the child develops:

0 – 6 or 7 years – a child is committed to their family and those people who care for them.

7 – 11 years - a child starts to form their own identity and becomes aware; they also have an opinion and want to be heard.

11 – 13 or 14 years – a child, now a young adult, will show different attitudes to different situations and may become opinionated about their own beliefs and boundaries.

14 – 25 years – the young adult will want to try different experiences and may test their environment; it can be a stressful time for loved ones or those onlookers such as grandparents, siblings, and close people within the family.

Facing the differences between the ages of 13 – 14 and up until 25 years can be daunting without a child being guided through that time. It has been seen in many generations, how customs and traditions within many cultures, have been established over many thousands of years, and how to help both children and their parents cope over these times.

Having said the above, maturity and development in some, and or in many females, may come at an earlier age than males! Estrogen levels, personality structure and life experiences all play their part in how, and when a young female becomes a mature adult.

Life experiences and how a person is treated as a child all influence the formation of the brain, the personality creation, and the behaviours shown as the young adult matures.

From my own experiences, the ages from 14 years through to about 25 years seem to be the most stressful for a parent. Not only as parents, do we struggle with our own emotions and of letting go, and letting go we must, our children may take on the world as if there is no tomorrow; they test, test and test, sometimes with negative results and then still test again!

LET'S RECAP

In the first two books: Changes Facing Kian and Changes Facing Rosie, I introduced the children to eight different hormones, the growth hormone (hGH), estrogen, progesterone, testosterone, estrone, estradiol, estriol and ghrelin.

The hormones within our bodies help to keep us healthy and allow us to live our daily lives. Hormones are essential if the body is to perform different movements, make different choices and to let us know when to eat, drink, fight, or flight; they are an essential part of the living system in animals, insects, and human beings.

To grow and be healthy, we need HGH within our body. When your body grows, you know you are getting older and growing into an adult.

HGH works with the other hormones we have spoken about. None of the hormones working to keep you healthy, can function properly, if you don't eat the correct food that your body identifies. Your food is the primary source of nutrition that feeds your hormones. When hormones have good food, so does your nervous system, your brain and body.

Testosterone, both males and females produce testosterone in their body, but males generally make more than females.

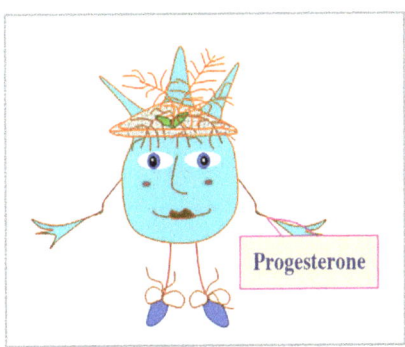

Progesterone is a hormone produced and released from the female ovaries. It helps when females start to have their periods and they help in the body's control of the menstrual cycle.

Estrone can store estrogen and helps with female development and plays a part in female reproductive health. Like most hormones, these work with your body's clock. Many hormones can be sensitive to your body changes. An example may be seen with severe dieting without medical advice or guidance.

Estriol, like estrone, and estradiol, helps the female body to grow and become ready for womanhood. Like so many hormones, it too, works with its own clock and will click into gear when it receives certain messages from your brain.

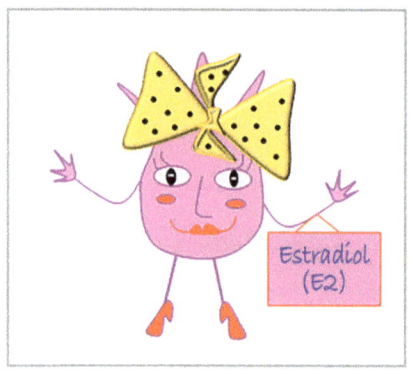

Estradiol is also a female hormone, produced primarily in the female ovaries. Estradiol levels can vary depending on the phase of the female menstrual cycle. Males also produce estradiol in their body.

Estrogen is the name given to a group of hormone compounds. It is a main hormone and is essential to the menstrual cycle which can go from twenty-one to thirty-five days. Estrogen helps a girl's body to mature. It also helps to make the bones stronger, and to keep the heart and brain healthy.

Women and girls have three types of hormones that work within the reproductive menstrual cycle: estrogen, estradiol and estriol. Estrogen binds together estradiol and estriol. Both males and females have this hormone.

Ghrelin is the hormone that lets you know when you feel hungry. If people eat when they are not hungry, for instance, junk food can make you feel full and about an hour later after the meal, you feel hungry again. This is when your ghrelin hormone is being overridden by the food additives in junk and processed food!

Hormones work as communication transmitters and can switch different chemicals on or off within the body and brain.

To give you some idea of this, when a tiny baby is hungry,

the hunger message is sent from the child's stomach to its brain. Ghrelin is thought to be produced in the stomach and has a direct communication route to the brain, a bit like a telecom's transmitter! The message is sent from the stomach through the nervous system that runs along the spine, to the brain. The reaction comes from the baby by the sound of the cry it makes!

The sound of the cry allows a mother to instantly understand the message, 'I am hungry!'

NOW, MORE HORMONES THAN YOU REALISE!

INTRODUCTION

This is the second book in the series of two books for girls, the first is 'Changes' Facing Rosie, now we bring to you, 'Changes' Facing Caitlin.

This is a story about a twelve-year-old girl, who is a paraplegic and lives in Northern Ireland; who has dreams and ambitions to be in the future Paralympic Games.

As a toddler, she and her family were in a train accident, Caitlin was the only one injured. After several operations on part of her lower left leg and foot to save them; it could not be done and was eventually amputated.

Both her parents were in the army at the time; after the accident, her mother resigned and stayed at home to look after Caitlin. Within a few months, her father who was a pilot, also died in another and second tragic accident.

Both Caitlin and her mum live with Caitlin's grandmother, Grandma Shirley, and being of a determined nature, Caitlin was not going to let part of a missing leg and foot stop her from doing anything she wanted to do!

She had a great circle of friends, many of them were athletic like Caitlin and her school also encouraged sport and many activities such as archery, netball, swimming, girls' football and cricket and many other curriculum and none-curriculum activities.

Caitlin's grandmother is Caitlin's biggest fan; she encourages Caitlin to do more sports activities than she is already doing. It is only Caitlin's mum who says, *'Mum, I think Caitlin has enough to do, and don't forget she has schoolwork too!'*

As a treat for Caitlin's thirteenth birthday, Shirley had bought four tickets for the Commonwealth Games in Birmingham, 2022. Caitlin was allowed to take one friend with them to the games, so she chose, Molly, her best friend.

Chapter One
The Birmingham Games 2022

Despite the prosthetic leg and foot, Caitlin did not miss an opportunity to play sport. She loved playing netball, cricket, football but most of all, she loved swimming. Her best friend Molly was also a keen swimmer, but Molly wasn't keen on playing any of the ball sports like Caitlin!

When Shirley, on Caitlin's thirteenth birthday, gave her granddaughter an envelope and when Caitlin opened it, she announced, '...we have four tickets for the Commonwealth Games, next year! She looked at her Gran, then her Gran replied, 'this is your birthday present from me, what do you think Caitlin?' Unable to believe what she had read from within the message within the envelope, which said, 'Welcome to the Commonwealth Games, 2022. Please find your four tickets enclosed.'

Caitlin's Gran was standing in the kitchen doorway, she was holding a potato and potato scraper while she watched her granddaughter's face of excitement and disbelief!

After a while, Caitlin looked again at the envelope's contents and said, 'Gran, there are four tickets but there are only three of us!' Caitlin waits for an answer from her Gran, then her Gran replies, 'Well, I thought it would be nice for you to take one of your friends with you and I would imagine, it would be Molly, am I right...?'

She replies to her Gran's question, '*Yes, of course, but I will have to ask her parents' first, they might say, "No" and I only want to ask Molly if her parents agree first; I will ask her after I've asked her parents...!*'

Gran looks at her granddaughter and nods her head in agreement.

The Games were still about fifteen months away, and nobody knew if there was going to be another outbreak of Covid when everything would be locked down again, so it was with caution that Caitlin set her sights on the Birmingham Games!

With her birthday being last Wednesday, it was now Saturday, and it was Caitlin's birthday party! Regardless of her prosthetic leg and foot, Caitlin had decided to have a pool party!

She could invite ten friends; these could include girls and boys. With her invitations given out over a week ago, all the friends meet at the doors of the Aquatic Centre. Once inside, the boys went to their cubicles to change and the girls to theirs.

Most of Caitlin's friends knew she had a prosthetic limb but one boy, Caitlin had not mentioned this fact! On seeing Caitlin in her swimsuit, she could see him looking at her stumpy leg. She asked him, '...*didn't you know I had a prosthetic limb?*' He looked back at her and answered, '*No', I didn't'*. His next question was, '*were you born like that, or did it happen through an accident?*' She replied, '*it happened through an* accident when I was a baby, but it doesn't worry me and besides, I'm not here at my birthday party to talk about my leg, I'm here to have fun with my friends', then she states, '...beat you into the pool!'

With that, she takes off, at the edge of the pool, she beats the boy, diving headfirst into the water!

Normally, running and diving wasn't allowed at the pool, but as it was just a few steps, Caitlin dared her chances in the short race with the boy...!

Caitlin's mum had organised the pool meeting with afternoon tea spent at the pizza shop and then a trip to the cinema for everybody. It was a great birthday, but now it was time to get back into her schoolwork as she rode her bike, to meet Molly on the way at the shops, and then on to school the next Monday morning!

With such a big weekend, Caitlin was still thinking, 'it was the best birthday ever and to think, we're going to the Birmingham Games next year!'

Meeting Molly on the way, Molly too, was still excited about the birthday party, so as the girls rode their bikes to school, each talked nonstop about the event.

The bell sounded as the girls chained their bikes up in the bike rack. They walked into the assembly hall where all the students meet each day. They had their names called out and the roll book was marked. After that, all the students made their way to their selected courses.

Caitlin's first lesson was math; she liked math, but she found her mind would wonder while she should be concentrating. With her birthday party still firmly in her mind, she found she couldn't help but look out of the classroom window while trying to do her schoolwork!

Her teacher, Mr O'Connor, called, *'Caitlin Murphy, why are you daydreaming today, you are not paying attention and have not heard a word I've said!'* Caitlin, realising she had been daydreaming most of the lesson, tried, now to concentrate on the work she had missed!

With a little concentration, she was able to catch up and at the end of the lesson, handed in her work to Mr O'Connor. As she did so, Mr O'Connor, asked, *'Where were you off to Caitlin, you were daydreaming and that is not like you?'* Before she could answer, Mr O'Connor continued, *'We have another lesson on Wednesday and I want your full concentration!'* Caitlin looked at her teacher and apologised for her actions, replying, *'I'm sorry, I will do better next Wednesday, Mr O'Connor!'*

The next lesson was biology and then sport, this was her favourite time of the school week. She paid attention all through biology and kept her notes and sketches up to date; she again, handed in her work to her teacher. This teacher was Mrs Sheerer, and Caitlin liked her very much.

Mrs Sheerer, was taking the next of Caitlin's lessons, sport, so Caitlin was looking forward to that. The lesson always started with some warmup exercises and then a sport, today was netball. Caitlin is an exceptional goalie and is always rostered to that position.

With their netball kit on, the girls made their way onto the pitch. It was a great game and lots of excitement as the goals stay the same; it was the closing minutes, and suddenly, Caitlin had the ball, could she score the one extra goal needed to win the game?

The game was intense with a lot of focus on this last shot, and Caitlin could feel the pressure, one, two three, with a perfect shot, she managed to score the needed goal and did it…!

Meanwhile, Molly's mum not only owned a very nice café in town, but she worked in it nearly every day. The cakes, and baking done on the premises, as anybody walked past the door, would smell so good, you would have to treat yourself to a very tasty treat! Caitlin's mum and grandmother would agree on this point!

Molly and Caitlin were on their bikes and riding home after school, when Molly said, *'I'm calling in to see my mum at the café, would you like to come in with me and I'm sure when mum hears how you won the netball game with that amazing goal you scored, she will give us both some afternoon tea!'*

Caitlin wasn't really thinking about afternoon tea, but just the mention of it made her mouth water, she knew that a delicious cake or treat would be in store and 'that was just too good to resist', she thought!

Caitlin nods her head to her friend in agreement, and realising it was later in the day, she replies, *'That sounds great, I wonder what beautiful cakes your mum has left?'* Molly replies, *'mum always has something for her special customers that she keeps hidden away!'*

With the thought of a delicious afternoon tea, the girls continue to ride their bikes, they went down a country lane, up a small hill that went over the train line and into town. Molly looks at Caitlin and says, *'I love this time of year and now that winter has gone, the flowers are coming out!'* She points to the flowers on the side of the road and says, *'...look at those daffodils over there, Caitlin!'*

Caitlin, slows her bike ride down, stops to look at the newly blooming flowers and says, *'they are very beautiful, I don't know if I have ever noticed these before!'* She also takes the opportunity to re-tie her laces of her shoe as one had come undone during the ride!

Reaching the café, the girls leave their bikes resting on the large tree outside and where they could see them from inside the café. Molly's mum meets the girls as they enter, and Molly excitedly tells her mum about the great score in the netball game that Caitlin scored. Excitedly she says to her mum, *'Mum, you should have seen this goal, it was right on the edge of the circle, and she did it, a perfect goal, just amazing...!'*

Molly's mum looks at both girls, and replies, *'Well, that deserves a treat and I think we might have something* special, a new type of cake that we have been working on. It is made of raspberries and flour, baked and then a new Italian custard we have been working to create. I'll ask Sharon to prepare these for you; and what would you like to drink, maybe a chocolate milkshake would be a good celebration drink, what do you girls think?'*

Caitlin, takes a minute, she could already taste the treat, and replies, *'That would be lovely, thank you!'*

The girls sit at a table and make themselves comfortable and wait for the tasty treats to arrive. Caitlin thinks to herself, 'I might make the excuse to go to the bathroom and ask Molly's mum about the Birmingham Games next year!'

She hadn't said anything to Molly about her birthday treat from her gran, Shirley, but this might be the perfect opportunity to do so! Politely, she says to Molly, *'I'm just going to the bathroom, Molly, I won't be long!'*

Molly, meanwhile, is searching through her diary looking for something, and isn't really concentrating on anything other than finding her lost information!

All the time, the beautiful smells of baking and cake making linger in the café's atmosphere, this gives the feeling of comfort and enjoyment of the treats to eat and enjoy!

Caitlin, goes to the bathroom as she has mentioned to Molly, but then diverts to the kitchen where she finds

Molly's mum and Sharon preparing their afternoon treat, Caitlin, on seeing the surprise, quickly says, *'Oh my, are those for us?'* Molly's mum looks at her in surprise at seeing Caitlin in the kitchen, and replies, *'...they are indeed, and very much deserved young lady!'*

After seeing such cake creations, and taking a chance to collect her thoughts, Caitlin, tells Molly's mum about her birthday gift of the tickets to the Birmingham Games and how she has one extra ticket and asks, *'Could I ask if Molly can come with us to the Games?'*

Molly's mum looks at the young girl's face looking at her with her large blue eyes, waiting in anticipation, of the mother's reply, Molly's mum then says, *'With me it is fine, but I will ask her dad if it is OK also, but I'm sure he will say "Yes"'*. Now, with the question asked, Caitlin joins her friend at the table to wait for their afternoon treats to arrive!

Molly was sitting quietly at the table when Caitlin arrives, and Caitlin asks, *'...did you find what you were looking for?'*

'Oh, yes', Molly replies, *'...it's these...!'* Showing Caitlin her class crumpled handouts from a few weeks ago, when Molly asks, *'...did you get these?'* Caitlin looks at the images looking back at her, and replies, *'No, where did you get those from?'*

Molly replies, *'...from Mrs Sheerer, she will probably give you them at the next lesson then!'*

The images sit on the café table as Molly's mum and Sharon bring out the very special afternoon tea.

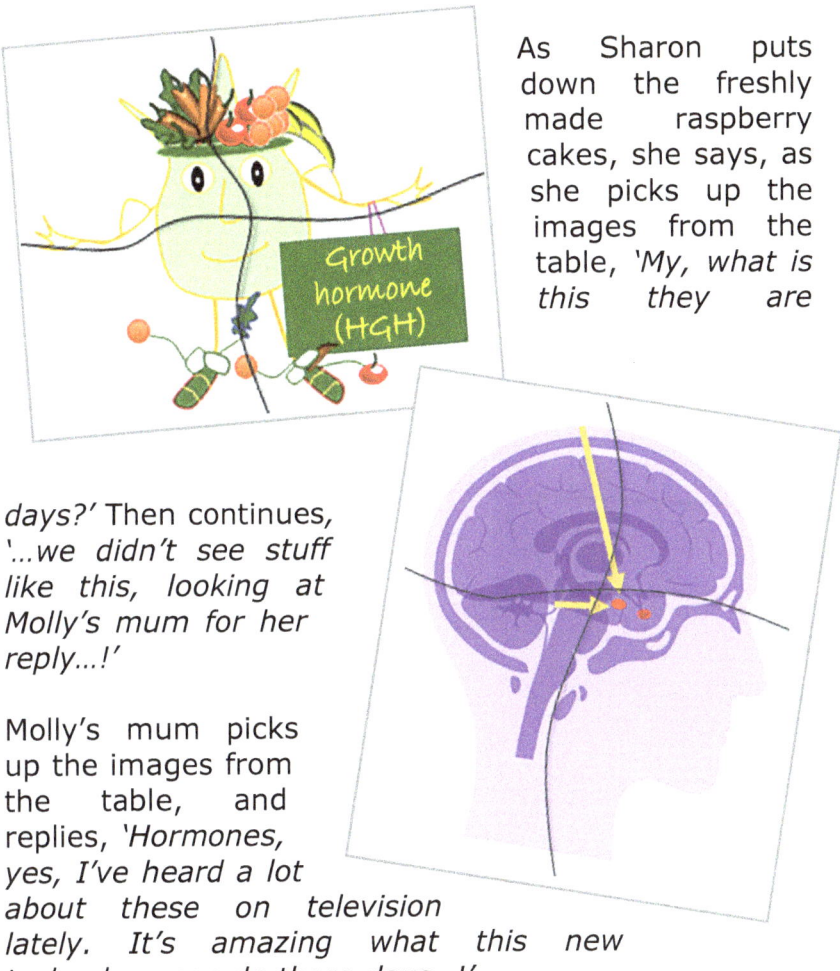

As Sharon puts down the freshly made raspberry cakes, she says, as she picks up the images from the table, 'My, what is this they are days?' Then continues, '...we didn't see stuff like this, looking at Molly's mum for her reply...!'

Molly's mum picks up the images from the table, and replies, 'Hormones, yes, I've heard a lot about these on television lately. It's amazing what this new technology can do these days...!'

She puts the sheets back down on the table and with that, the two women turned around and went back into the kitchen to finish off making the new raspberry cakes! At the table, Molly and Caitlin couldn't believe the delight of the tastes they were experiencing...!

Molly, fossicked through her bag to find another book, and eventually at the bottom of the bag, pulls out another exercise book and says to Caitlin, '...*have you seen these before?*' She then pulls out her battered exercise book from the previous term!

Caitlin looks at the images on the book, and replies to Molly, '*No, I've never seen these before, where did you get them?*' Molly replies, '*From Sonya, she did this subject last year....!*'

Chapter Two
A surprising interaction

Having seen the images shown by Molly at the café a few days earlier, Caitlin had seen the growth hormone image previously and knew a little about that hormone, but she had not seen the image of the head before.

It was the day of the lesson with Mrs Sheerer, and the images were given out together with the class objectives for the lesson.

Molly was learning the piano and did not attend this lesson!

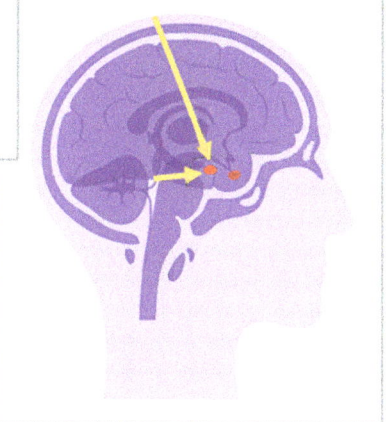

With both images sitting on their desks, Mrs Sheerer says as she starts her lesson, '...*did you know,* '...*that everybody has hormones working inside their body and not only their body but also their brain?'*

Like most thirteen-year-old teenagers, Caitlin had

never thought much about hormones and how they work in the body. She was attentive to what the teacher was speaking about when Mrs Sheerer continues, *'I'm now introducing you to the growth hormone. Some of you may be familiar with this hormone as I did speak to a group of students last week about this!'* She continues, *'...some children may have learnt about this in their primary school, but if so, we will just go over some information and bring everybody up to speed, so that you all learn together!'*

She continues, *'the reason we grow, is because of this hormone, all animals, including insects, plants and trees have growth hormones, or a chemical that allows them to grow!'*

The girl sitting behind Caitlin puts up her hand and Mrs Sheerer, stops what she is saying, asking the girl, *'Would you like to speak Anna?* Anna replies, *'Yes, Mrs Sheerer, if we don't have growth hormones in our body, would we stop growing?'* Mrs Sheerer, says back to the class, *'that is a good question.* She stops, and thinks, then replies, *"yes" we would stop growing and probably without growth hormones, we would not exist!'*

'Wow', one boy replies, *'that is really scary Miss, and to think that we all need that hormone because it allows us to grow; does that mean Miss'.* He continues with his question, *''that when we were conceived, that the growth hormone was already in our body, it's not something that happened later?'* Mrs Sheerer, thinks

and gives the boy quality time because of the depth of thinking he is doing!

He is going back to before his birth with how he is thinking, Mrs Sheerer, too, thinks about her student's last comment and then remarks, '...*that is a really good question Simon and thank you for thinking so deeply.*'

With that last comment, Mrs Sheerer asks the rest of the class, '*Would anybody like to add their comment?*' Caitlin, hesitant to ask her question, puts her hand up and then stands, she says, '*My grandmother, Shirley, says that hormones start to change in the boy and girl's body at about the age of seven to eight, is that correct Mrs Sheerer?*' Mrs Sheerer takes her time to answer, and then replies, '*Yes, all the children around the world will start to experience little changes in their body, and the way they think. All of you have gone past that stage, but if you have brothers or sisters of that similar age, they will now start to change. They may start to want to take more control over what they do; they may want to have their private time to themselves, and you may have noticed other behaviours that are very different from the time of when they were a baby!*'

As the class became interested in the different information, more hands went up and so a lively debate continued within the group!

Mrs Sheerer still had a lot of information to get through, and then said to her class, '*We must move on as there are over fifty hormones in your body; we will not have time to discuss all of them, but you do need* to know about the hormones that are working in your bodies and those hormones will turn you into young men and women!'

When she heard Mrs Sheerer's last words, they struck Caitlin, she had thought before about growing up, but she had never thought about becoming a 'young woman!'

She was now eager to know and continually asked the question inside her head, 'what is the difference between being a girl or being a woman?'

Mrs Sheerer was keen to move on and referred the class back to their handout and points to the image on the screen.

She continues and says, 'Thank you for your lively discussion and the information we have shared, we now know that we need the growth hormone (HGH) it allows us to grow and become adults. Now we need to look at how this happens. There are hormones in many parts of your body, including your brain; there are also areas of your brain that release different hormones, at different times, that work as triggers and these also go to different parts of your body; these triggers, help other hormones to work!'

One boy says out loud, *'WoW', that seems very complicated to me, Miss!'* Mrs Sheerer, nodded her head and in reply she says, *'...it is but, you will understand more as we move on!'*

She continues, *'your brain is a marvellous piece of human technology; we often think of computers and cars as having technology, but your brain is indeed advanced "human technology" and has taken millions of years to be the brain you have inside your head today!'*

She then says, *'...to allow people and animals to grow, and for the species to survive, they must grow to maturity. All growing things need a growth hormone for this to happen.'* She takes a breath, while pointing at the image on the screen and continues, *'The growth hormone, which we've see on the screen, is a naturally occurring hormone produced by the pituitary gland, it stimulates growth into maturity in children and young adults during adolescents. The pituitary gland sits in and works from the middle of your brain.'*

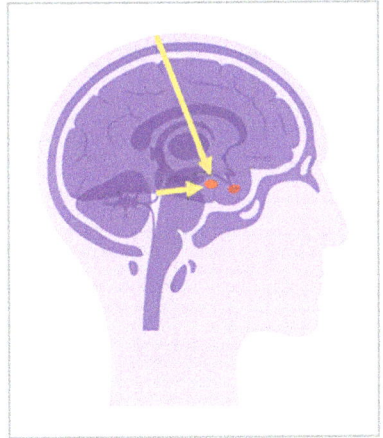

She then says, *'If you put your finger, and in your mind, think of a line on top and in the middle of your head, and then imagine where the front of your ear is, then think about meeting the two lines, within your brain, you will*

roughly understand where the two lines meet and is where your pituitary gland sits within your brain!

Let's look at this image again!'

The teacher stopped speaking while the students did the exercise of trying to draw the imaginary lines with their fingers from their ears to the middle of their heads!

There were about thirty students in the room and with each student working from the top of their heads to their front of their ears, the laughter and good learning being done was great for the teacher to see.

Caitlin was enjoying the lesson and now knew why Molly was determined to find the handouts at the café she had been given in her lesson.

After the last school bell rang for the day, Molly and Caitlin meet in the bike shed. Molly quickly tells Caitlin, *'I'm calling in to see Grandma Tickner at the farm on the way home, do you want to come with me?'* Caitlin thinks, and replies, *'...that would be great, and I'd love to see the new lambs that have just arrived, but I will have to let my mum and Shirley know otherwise they will worry!'*

Caitlin had been given a new phone for her birthday and it was to be used for precisely these times. The phone had limited use with only contacts permitted by her mum, everything else was restricted!

The two girls rode to the farm. The farm was open to the public at certain times of the year where the young animals, recently born, could be seen, and petted.

Down winding lanes and over the hill, they rode their bikes, when eventually they both saw, the old farmhouse with its yellowish walls in the distance.

On reaching the farmhouse, the girls left their bikes at the front, heavy wooden door, and went into the building. Grandma Tickner, saw the girls as they walked into the kitchen and dropped everything she had in her hands, to go to and hug them.

In the greetings that were exchanging, the girls hadn't seen the young woman sitting on the chair by the hearth! Grandma Tickner, said to Molly, *'...did you know your cousin, Sheena is here, she's taking a break from her work at the university to come and see us?'*

Then, from out of the shadows of the fire and the corner of the room, the young woman stepped forward.

Sheena introduced herself to Caitlin and Molly and says to Molly, *'My, you have grown, you were just a little baby when I saw you last; I nursed you to sleep; you were having a very restless time...!* Sheena, then held Molly tightly as she recalled the memories of the tiny baby.

On Sheena's release, Molly stood back and introduced Caitlin to her cousin, saying *'this is Caitlin, she is my best friend!'*

Grandma Tickner put the kettle on to make some tea, asking, 'do you girls drink tea or do you drink that rubbish I see so many young people drinking?' Grandma Tickner was known for the honesty of her thoughts, and she would always let people know if she didn't agree with something…!

Grandma Tickner and Sheena prepared the afternoon tea of homemade butter cake and hot tea. 'It was very good' thought Caitlin as she ate the cake and sipped the tea!

Sheena was eager to hear about the subjects the girls were doing at school, and said, 'Well, tell me about your schoolwork and what are you two girls really interested in?'

Molly, while swallowing her last piece of butter cake quickly said, 'We're just starting to learn about hormones and how important they are for your body…!'

'Goodness,' was the reply from Sheena, 'I only learnt about hormones when I went to university and that's some time ago now…!' She continues and asks, 'and what do you know about hormones?' Caitlin replies, 'we know that everything that grows needs to have growth hormones, even plants, insects and people otherwise they won't grow….!' Then Molly replies, '…yes, we'll die…!'

Grandma Tickner, was not a part of the conversation, and as she stands up from sitting on her chair at the table during afternoon tea, she replies, '…well, you *learn something new every day, I didn't learn about hormones when I was at school, just reading, writing and arithmetic, that's all they knew then...!'*

Chapter Three
Sheena takes the girls' home

Sheena, helps Grandma Tickner with tidying up the teacups and cake plates, and then says to Molly, *'Have you come to see your Uncle Patrick and Uncle Michael, if so, they are all out with the animals?'* As Sheena speaks, Molly and Caitlin are helping with cleaning and removing cake crumbs from the table!

Sheena puts on her boots at the door, and says to Grandma Tickner, *'...are you coming over to see the newborn Granny?'* Grandma Tickner replies, *'Yes, I'll be there in a minute, I'll just wash these dishes and then join you...!'*

Sheena and the girls make their way to the barn where nursing ewes are looking after their lambs, some of the lambs are just born, while other ewes are giving birth!

Molly's Uncles, Patrick, and Michael are with the ewes while the uncles' wives are also helping. Caitlin says to Molly, *'there must be hundreds of lambs being born...!'* Uncle Patrick hears Caitlin's comment, and replies, *'...we have sixty-seven ewes in here at the moment, each is either in labour, given birth or about to give birth, so it is a very busy time for us farmers!'*

At that point, Grandma Tickner joins her sons in the barn and starts to give a hand. Some of the ewes were having problems, but the family was there to help them through their birthing time...!

The time was getting on and Caitlin started to worry, she says, *'I will have to go, mum and Shirley will be getting worried about me!'* Sheena, quickly says, *'I'll drive you girls back into town, I have my car here, and it will be easy to put your bikes in the back…!'*

Hearing this, Caitlin sends Shirley and her mum a message from her phone. She waits for a response, then says, *'Shirley says it's OK, I can stay a little longer!'*

With that, the girls stay a little longer on the farm. Sheena then takes the girls to see the new arrivals, they are the new baby lamas, *'…and only born last Friday…!'* says, Sheena.

On seeing the newborn lamas, Caitlin says, *'Oh, they are so cute!'* Molly also hadn't known about the young lamas…! Sheena then said, *'a young lama is called a crias, they are, "cute" as you said, Caitlin!'* Then Sheena reminded them of getting home before dark, saying, *'Girls, I had better get you home, your mothers' will be worrying!'*

With saying their *'goodbyes'* to the Tickner family and Grandma Tickner, reminding the girls, *'…don't leave it so long before we see you again, you are growing far too fast and before we know it, you too, will be off to college or university like Sheena…!'*

With the bikes loaded into the back of the car, Sheena drove the girls home. On the journey, Caitlin, asked, *'what do you do at the university Sheena?'* She replied,

I work as an endocrinologist, which means, *I work at the university and in a hospital. I am mainly interested in hormones and how they work in the human body...!'*

Molly was listening to the conversation, and she then said, '*...we are just learning about hormones, our hormones have funny hats...!'*

Sheena on hearing this, said, '*...really, none of my hormones wear hats, I would like to meet your hormones...!'* she then gives a little laugh and chuckle, and then repeats to the girls, *'hormones with hats....!'* And laughs again! She pauses, and continues, *'I'm staying at the farm for a while, while the birthing of the animals is taking place! How about, I speak to your mums', Molly, and Caitlin, maybe, we can all meet at your mum's café next week, what about Wednesday, after school?'*

To Caitlin, the suggestion from Sheena was perfect and she said, *'do you mind if I ask my Grandma Shirley also?'* Sheena laughed, and said, *'No, of course not, we can all meet up, besides, I haven't seen your grandmother and mother for a long time, possibly since before I went to university to do my studies, so that would be great to catch up!'*

With the date firmly fixed for the next meeting with Sheena, each girl was taken to her home and their bikes unloaded from the car. By the time Caitlin got home, she was excited and buzzing. Grandma Shirley had dinner ready, and Caitlin could hardly eat her meal, she was saying to her grandma and mum, '*...you should* see these baby lamas mum and Grandma, they are so cute, their real name as a baby, is crias, so they are not called lambs like baby sheep, but crias, they are just so cute! Also, Uncle Patrick says they have about sixty-seven ewes giving birth, have given birth or are in labour!' Grandma Shirley continues to eat her meal while she listens to the excitement of her granddaughter!

Caitlin continues, 'So, Grandma Shirley, both of you are invited to Molly's mum's café for afternoon tea next Wednesday, isn't that also great?'

The meal was over, Caitlin had a lot of schoolwork to do, but she was so excited about so many things that were happening, she didn't know if she had the energy to do much work!

For Revision: The first hormone we spoke about was the Growth, explain in one sentence what you know about this hormone
....
....
....

She helped with tidying up the table from the meal, said 'goodnight' to her mum and Grandma, had a shower and then went to her bedroom to unpack her school bag and to see the latest information that Mrs Sheerer had given to the class. As she gave out the handouts and worksheets, Mrs Sheerer had said, '...*now class, I want you to become familiar with the new terms of hormones and the way they look! We will go into more information in our next class...!*'

Caitlin looked at the work she needed to do. She went through the worksheets and scratched her head and said quietly, '*so much work and I've got so many things on at the moment and I must get back to my swimming training!*'

As she sat on her bed, her mind was racing, she couldn't help but think about the new lambs, the young crias at the farm and all the things that were going on at this one time!

For Revision: Estrogen is an important hormone for females, can you, in one sentence, tell us why?
....
....
....

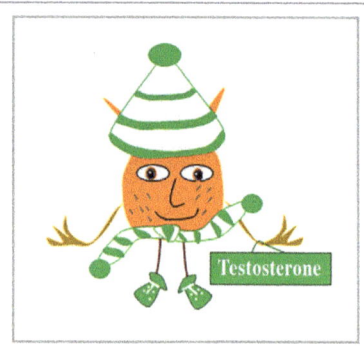

For Revision: Testosterone is in both males and females, in one sentence can you tell us why is this?
....
....
....

She also felt very tired, and her bed, it looked so good and felt so soft, she couldn't help but stop, lie down, and take a little rest, '...then get up and do her homework!' she thought...!

When she woke, she got up, moved the curtains back and looked out of her bedroom window, she was shocked, the sun was coming up, it was a new day! She also quickly looked across her bedroom floor at all the undone schoolwork!

She, again, looked at the sheets on her bedroom floor, they were as she had left them the night before! She then looked at her clock, it was only six-forty-five!

'There was still time to do some schoolwork!' she thought! She looked at the sheets again, and noticed two had **For Revision**, written on them, she knew those answers and quickly worked on those! She then looked at the three remaining sheets, which had nothing written on them, so she left those.

Having her schoolwork finished, she had a shower, dressed in her school uniform, made her bed, and was ready for school!

She went downstairs where Grandma Shirley had set the table and was busy scrambling some eggs for Caitlin's mum's breakfast. Grandma Shirley, looked at her granddaughter and said, '*My, haven't you slept all night, you look as tired as when you went to bed…?*'

Caitlin replies to her grandmother, '*After my shower Grandma Shirley, I sat on my bed, looked at my schoolwork and fell asleep, that's probably why I look tired!*'

While Grandma Shirley keeps stirring the eggs, she said again, '*…. probably too much going on for such a young head…!*'

With that, Caitlin's mum comes into the kitchen from the garden, and says to her mum, '...mum, I've fed the chickens, the ducks want more but they can swim in the pond, there's enough food in there to keep them happy! The cat's had kittens and produced four overnight! And the dog's had his breakfast, so all is well!

Caitlin's mum thinks again and says, 'Phebie, the cat is very protective and wasn't happy about me picking up her kittens; she's usually friendly and loves a pat and her breakfast, but as I picked up the first kitten, I could hear her give a little growl and grunt, that's not like her...!'

Grandma Shirley, said, 'I'll go and have a look at her after I've had my coffee and see what's the matter with her!'

After breakfast and quickly, and before school, Grandma Shirley and Caitlin go to see Phebie; on looking down at the cat, Grandma Shirley, says, 'she looks a bit poorly to me, I might get the vet to have a look at her and her kittens today...!'

On the way to school, Caitlin meets Molly at the café, where she quickly tells her about Phebie the cat and the kittens.

After chaining the bikes up in the bike rack, they make their way to assembly. After a short assembly, it was time to go to Mrs Sheerer's class. Caitlin felt glad she had done the revision but now she needed to find the worksheets to do her lessons on!

Mrs Sheerer came into the classroom and said to the students, *'Please get your worksheets out and we will talk about the hormones on the sheets and then we will go for sport, this time, we will play some cricket, but we need to complete the hormone sheets first! We will recap on the growth hormone, are there any questions and are you all familiar with this hormone?'* The slide of the growth hormone appears on the screen, and she asks, *'Can anybody tell me, what would happen if we did not have growth hormones in our bodies?'*

One boy puts his hand up, then stands behind his desk, and says, *'Miss, we would not grow, then we would probably die, Miss!'* Mrs Sheerer replies, *'Yes, excellent answer.'*

She then goes to the hormone testosterone, and asks, *'Do both males and females have testosterone?'* One boy and girl at the back of the class start to giggle, and Mrs Sheerer asks, *'...and David and Sarah, what is so funny about the question?'*

She waits patiently for an answer, but no answer is forthcoming!

Mrs Sheerer, then answers her own question, saying, '... we know that males and females produce testosterone, and we know that testosterone is a male hormone, and in biologically male bodies, there is more of this hormone than estrogen. Both boys and girls produce testosterone, but in girls, the amounts are smaller. Testosterone helps to build your muscles and helps to keep your bones strong, other benefits include, it helps to keep your brain healthy, and that is for both boys and girls...!'

She continues, 'The next slide I want to talk to you about is estrogen. Both males and females have estrogen. In biologically male bodies, estrogen is needed to balance testosterone.'

She takes a breath, then continues, '...estrogen also helps to protect your brain, it helps with your memory and in some of the fine jobs it helps the fine muscles in your fingers to work! Such jobs as decorating a cake or when you are doing fine craft projects, such as painting as in art; and with girls and women, it helps them when they put on their makeup!

When a man works on electrical projects, it helps to keep his hands steady when he's welding fine wires and so estrogen is very important in our everyday lives.

Estrogen also helps when a female's body is ready to make a baby, but as we all know, there are rules and regulations in our community that also need to be obeyed! Estrogen also helps in the growth of male sperm, so it has many jobs to do...!'

The next slide is on the screen and some students laugh at the strange hat; progesterone is wearing!
Mrs Sheerer continues, *'Progesterone is known as a master hormone. It is produced in the female ovaries and in the adrenal glands. It is an important hormone as it is necessary to produce estrogen and testosterone. It helps to stop depression, headaches, it also helps in keeping your bones and brain healthy!'*

Mrs Sheerer is aware of the time, and reminds the class, *'We just have two more hormones to discuss and then we will have our game of cricket.!'* She quickly adds, *'we do have a double session today, so we have plenty of time...!'*

'The next hormone', she says, *'...is adrenaline, having too much adrenaline in*

our bodies and brain can make us angry and leave us feeling tired. When we feel like this, we may want to fight with our siblings, cause a fight in the playground, be rude to mum and dad and the people we love. By doing the things we love to do, we can reduce adrenaline, and this makes us feel happy...!

She quickly wants to speak about gonadotropin, and says, 'Gonadotropins have a main function and that is to work with the gonads, meaning, the gonad is the sex or reproductive gland in both females and males.

The female reproductive cell are egg cells, and in males, the reproductive cells are sperm!'

With her last slide shown, the students go to their changing rooms and dress for their game of cricket.

Molly and Caitlin quickly stand together and chat on the cricket pitch, Mrs Sheerer sees the pair and sends Molly to one end of the pitch and Caitlin to the other until it was their turn to bat...!

Chapter Four
They all meet for afternoon tea

With so many things happening, including the Birmingham Games in the next few months, Caitlin had decided to go to the pool to train with her swimming on a regular weekly basis. Molly too, thought that was a great idea!

They had decided to go three times a week, they each spoke to their parents', and everybody also thought that was a good idea! Grandma Shirley suggested meeting up with a coach she had got to know at the Aquatic Centre! Grandma Shirley was a great swimmer and often went to the pool while her daughter was at work and Caitlin was at school!

With the new swimming dates in place, and a firm future set out by Grandma Shirley on the Monday, it was now Wednesday and time to meet for afternoon tea, with Sheena, Molly's mum and dad, Grandma Shirley, Caitlin's mum, Molly, and Caitlin, at Molly's mum's café.

With so many delicious cake aromas, it was difficult not to enjoy the venue. It was always very clean, with little old fashioned square windows at the front and side of the cafe building; these windows were polished and without a fingerprint! There were old-fashioned china and flowery patterned teapots with cups and saucers to match, fine teaspoons and forks and lace doylies all set out on the tables, and not to mention, the very clean lace tablecloths, that were always being washed by

Molly's mum, and clean on the tables; *'it is indeed, a very pretty café!'* Grandma Shirley would always say after a visit!

With the families having afternoon tea, Sheena says, *'One weekend, I would like to take the girls to the university to see where I work, and then on to the hospital to see the type of research I do with my colleagues on hormones, would it be possible for me to do that, and girls, would you like to do that…?'*

Caitlin was beaming, her face was so happy to see at such a suggestion. Molly too, was excited about the suggestion. Molly's mum said to her dad, *'what do you think, Ben, would you like Molly to go for such a visit?'* Ben replies, *'I think that would be grand…!'*

Caitlin sat quietly, while she waited to hear from her mum, then Caitlin's mum says, *'Caitlin, would you like to do that with Sheena?'* Caitlin, couldn't wait to reply, she then said, *'Mum, that would be awesome, to see a university and to see where research is done would just be awesome…!'*

With the parents agreeing, everything was in place for the girls to go on a visit to the university and hospital in Dublin.

Then Molly's mum says, *'we have another question to be answered'*, she then asks, *'Molly, would you like to go to the Birmingham Games with Caitlin, Grandma Shirley and Caitlin's mum?'* Molly looks at her mum, then Grandma Shirley, Caitlin's mum and then Caitlin, then replies, *'Oh mum, are you serious, of course, "yes" I would love to go to the Games!'*

So, two big questions had been asked, by this time, both Caitlin and Molly were so excited, they couldn't stop talking about the upcoming events.

With a large plate of beautifully decorated cakes, tea, coffee, and lemonade served on the table, the chatter and excitement from the table was loud!

The trip to Dublin would take place in two weeks' time and before the afternoon tea was over, Sheena said, *'be sure to bring your workbooks on hormones. You will then see how our work at the university ties in with what you are learning!'*

The weekend had come, and Sheena arrived exactly on time to pick up Caitlin and then on to the café, to meet and pick up Molly!

As Molly got into the vehicle, Sheena, asked, *'girls have you got your exercise books with your work on hormones?'* Both girls replied together, *'Yes', Sheena, we have them….!'*

It was late into the evening when the three arrived at Sheena's apartment in Dublin. Sheena had bought some frozen pizzas for dinner, earlier that week, with an extra jacket potato if the girls were still hungry; she also had strawberries and ice cream for dessert. With dinner over, the girls went to their bedroom; in the corner was a bunk bed, *'…one of you can sleep on the top and one of you can sleep on the bottom bunk, I will let you both sort out which bunk you want to sleep on!'* said Sheena.

Sheena showed the girls the bathroom and suggested, *'...it's time for bed, we have a big day tomorrow. We will go to the laboratory at the university in the morning and look at the research we are doing and then on to the hospital in the afternoon!'*

With the plates and dishes tidied away, the girls went to their bedroom. Sheena thought they would talk well into the night, but they did not. She looked in to see if they were asleep and they were. With that, Sheena too, went to bed.

The following morning the three were up early; after breakfast, Sheena said, *'let's have a look at your exercise books and you can show and tell me what you have been doing?'* With this, both the girls went to their bags and put their books on the table!

With the images and number of hormones on display, Sheena's reply was quick, *'Goodness, your teachers are very good to give you such information, I had to wait until I got to university to find out only half of this!'*

With an early breakfast over, and Sheena seeing the girls' work in their exercise books, it was time to go to the lab at the university.

As Sheena drove her car onto the university campus, she needed to show her ID Card at the gate, then the gate attendant, said, *'Nice to see you Dr Tickner;* he further asks, *'...working on a Saturday?'* She replies, *'No, Fred, just showing these two young ladies our work in the lab...!'* She then drove to her parking space.

Sheena parks the car and the three make their way to the building where Sheena works. Despite it being Saturday, *'...there were hundreds of students going in different directions; each seem to know exactly where they were going!'* thought Caitlin.

Then, Caitlin, takes some time to look at the magnificent old buildings! Molly too, is struck by what she is seeing. She says to Sheena, *'I had no idea you worked in such a place...!'* Sheena then replies, *'Yes, this university goes back to 1592, and the time of Queen Elizabeth the First!'*

Caitlin thinks, *'these buildings are so old and beautiful...!'*

Molly then said, *'is Saturday always busy like this?'* Sheena replies, *'early in the semester it's not this bad but as we get closer to the exam time, students start to panic and want to work every minute of the day; some do too much work and are so tired when it comes to exam time, they cannot work because they are exhausted!'* She stops what she is saying as a large group of students walk right in front of the three, the three stop in their tracks, to let the talking and laughing students pass them...!

In the lab, Sheena shows the girls the different types of hormones and explains, *'did you know, there are over fifty hormones in your body, and we think even more will be discovered in the future?'*

Molly replies, *'Yes, Mrs Sheerer, has said that at the beginning of the term!'* Then Caitlin replies, *'Mrs Sheerer has said, hormones are messengers and send messages to different parts of your body...!'* Sheena then replies, *'that is true. When your hormones aren't balanced, you can feel sad, angry and have other feelings. Some hormones are also very good, and they let you know when you feel happy!'*

They were now at the lab door; Sheena opens the door to reveal an area of research that Molly or Caitlin had not seen before. There were different formulas and calculations written on chalkboards and other areas had different formulas displayed showing different areas of research!

Molly went one way and Caitlin the other! Both girls were intrigued by what they saw!

With the lab visit over, the three headed to the refectory for lunch, that afternoon was the trip to the hospital!

Chapter Five
Learning more about hormones

Having had a very nice meal of meatballs and rice at the university refectory, the three were now back in another lab at the hospital.

This was a very different lab with many benches, computers, and chairs where people sat when they were working. Sheena explains, *'because it is the weekend, we only have a few people working; there is always someone here during the day, and sometimes, if we are rostered on, we may come in to work during the night; that's not very often! It's only if there are pandemics, like with Covid!'* She further explains, *'different sections of the lab specialise in different research, that is why you can see the different screens separating each section!'*

Molly, is thinking and then says, *'Is that so you don't get contamination of the work?'* Caitlin and Sheena, both look at Molly, then Caitlin replies, *'how did you know about that?'* Molly replies, *'I saw something on a television documentary and found it interesting!'*

Then Sheena says, as she walks with the girls to a large table. Sheena calls it the *'stainless steel table'*, then she says, *'Let's continue our discussion on hormones!'* Reaching the table, she pulls out three stools from under the table and signals for the girls to sit down, one each side of her! Then she says, *let's now look at some more hormones!' I was speaking to Mrs Sheerer, and told her, you were both coming to the university and hospital with me this weekend, and she thought it was a good idea! She has given me some more hormone images to talk about with you!'

She speaks, as she looks at the images in front of

her, *'There are quite a number here…!'*

The girls also have their workbooks open, so there is a lot of work for Sheena to see, as the three head into their discussion.

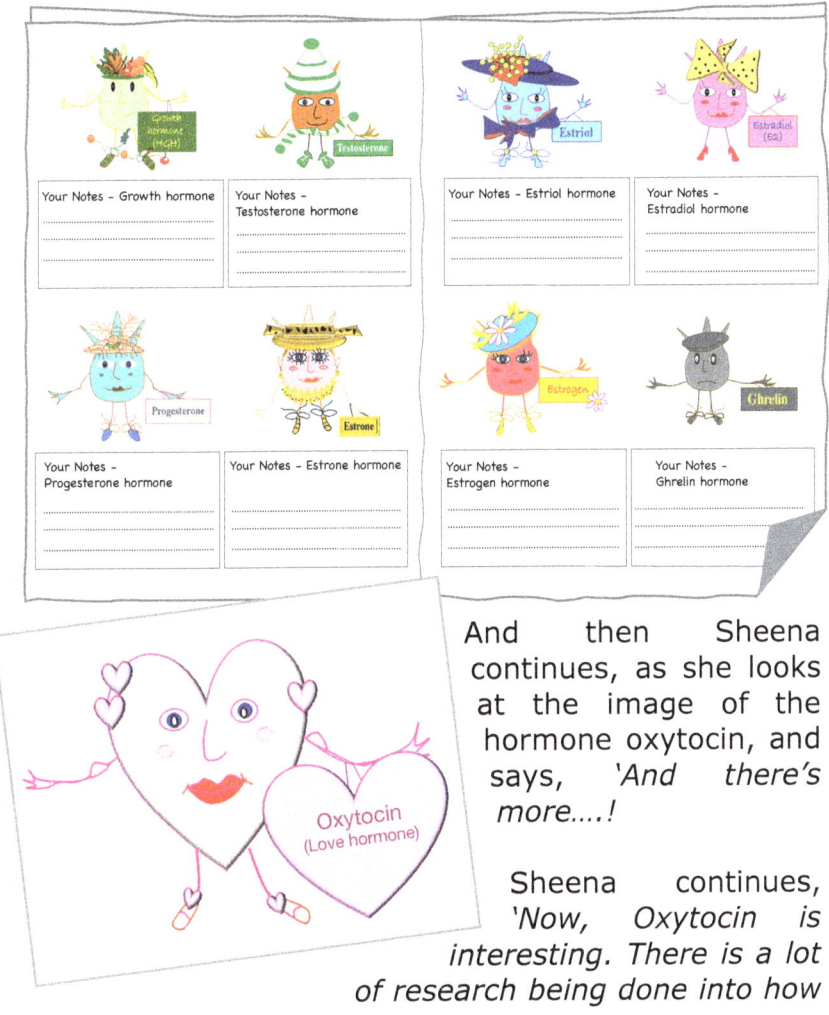

And then Sheena continues, as she looks at the image of the hormone oxytocin, and says, *'And there's more….!'*

Sheena continues, *'Now, Oxytocin is interesting. There is a lot of research being done into how* this hormone works! We now know that when people are sad, there is less oxytocin being produced in the brain, therefore, this leads to some people to experience depression and other feelings of loneliness!'

She stops, takes a breath, and says, 'that's why it is always important to have a project, play sport or have other interests that are yours!'

Sheena takes her time as she looks at both images of dopamine, then she says to the girls, 'When there are high levels of dopamine in your body, your brain is telling you to party!

This is not always a good thing! Many people who take drugs or have other bad habits that are not good for their body or brain may have larger quantities of dopamine in their body's system!' So, now let's go back to the hormones on this table and have a closer look at what they do...!

Sheena continues, '*when you have low dopamine, you can feel sad!*'

Sheena then says to Caitlin, '*Caitlin, what do you understand about adrenaline?*' Caitlin replies, '*I know that adrenaline is released into your body when you are frightened, and or when you are scared, like being in bed at night and you hear the tree branches tap your bedroom window when the wind blows, Sheena, that sends freaks down my spine….!*'

Before Caitlin could finish, Molly wants to talk to add her bit of information. She says, '*Yes, Sheena, I was riding my bike the other day and it was getting dark, I thought I saw shapes moving in the bushes, it made me ride faster and faster….!*' Sheena quietly replies, '*goodness, that would have been frightening, are you OK now?*' Molly nods her head in response…!

Sheena continues, '*So, to keep the levels of adrenaline at a good level in your body, you can do some deep breathing exercises, again, play some sport, turn off devices, such as your phone, an hour before you go to bed, or simply read a good book that is not going to frighten the daylights out of you; all these techniques help to lessen adrenaline!*'

As Caitlin sees Sheena lift the paper image from the other images, she says, '*I know that this hormone is*

called a stress hormone which helps my body change when I'm frightened, I know that cortisol carries different messages to different parts of my body, so if I'm frightened, this hormone sends a message to my legs to peddle faster, as Molly would have done when she thought she saw the shapes in the bushes move, when she was riding her bike the other night….!' Caitlin, then adds, '*She peddled herself out of danger!*'

Sheena, looks at both girls, and says, '*that is an excellent answer, Caitlin, and thank you for that…!*'

Sheena then adds to the information, '*…each day, cortisol, has several roles or jobs it does to keep your body healthy. It helps to regulate your blood pressure, that is how fast or slow your blood is moving around your body, it also helps you to learn and form new memories that are stored in your brain; it helps you to digest your food and manages how your body works to separate the protein, fat, or carbohydrate in the food you eat. So, it is not only a stress hormone, but it is an important hormone that helps your body to stay healthy.*'

Molly was thinking and Sheena could see she was deep in thought, she asks Molly, *'and Molly, what are you thinking about?'*

Molly replies, *'I was thinking about how cortisol helps your body to digest your food, Sheena, and how it helps it separates the protein, fat and carbohydrates!'* She stops and then continues, *'…what are carbohydrates, Sheena?'*

Sheena thinks and then replies, *'…there are two types of carbohydrate, one, is complex carbohydrate such as eating an apple or a slice of whole grain bread; these are good carbohydrates, and your body likes these. The other is processed carbohydrate which is found in all processed food such as doughnuts, processed and takeaway food, many ice creams, and many other foods; your body does not like these! You may like the taste in your mouth, but your body will eventually reject these carbohydrates by making you sick, overweight or with some other illness!'*

Sheena thinks, then says, *'We know that cortisol and adrenaline are the hormones that make us move faster or do quicker actions, but sometimes we make too much of both of these hormones, have you got any idea of what this does to your body and brain?'*

Caitlin, has a go at answering the question, *'Well, I would think you could become very stressed because that is not natural…!'* Then Molly says, *'I wouldn't like to feel like that all the time, like the time of riding my* bike the other night, like I did! I could feel my heart thumping and it frightened me!'

Sheena replied, 'No, that is not good, and we all need to be aware of those feelings and reactions and how to manage them...!'

Sheena continues and says, '...as I have said before, 'To keep your body and brain balanced, it is good to play sport, have hobbies, or do the good things you like doing; these can help to keep your body's system balanced. When you enjoy the things you do, your body and brain are happy...! Besides, when we have too much adrenaline, or cortisol in our body, we can feel angry, frustrated, short tempered and we are not nice to be with. We lose our friends and can become thoroughly miserable!

You can see in this image, as Sheena points with her finger, '...cortisol is happier, the colour of his face is lighter and you can see he has a smile, he looks so much happier than the cortisol image on the other page...!'

Then Sheena moves to the next image in front of her, and asks, 'what do you know about this head, it may even resemble how your head looks on the inside...!'

She continues and says, 'Many hormones are triggered by the pituitary gland, and Mrs Sheerer has said, you have done the exercise where you measured your head to find out where this gland sits inside your brain!'

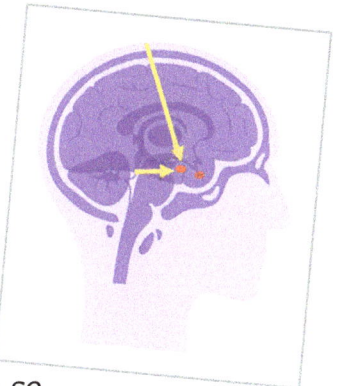

Caitlin replies, '...that was funny, some of the boys took it so seriously, they were trying to measure their heads with their rulers, set squares and any other thing they could measure with...!' Both girls giggle as they remember the boys and the actions they took during the exercise!

Sheena joins in the fun and says, 'it would have been funny to see those boys trying to measure their heads...!'

Both girls reply, 'It was very funny Sheena...!'

Sheena now pulls gonadotropin into the top of the pile of papers, then asks the girls, 'What do you know about gonadotropin girls?' Molly says, 'Well, Mr White, our art teacher, says that green represents, growth and the time to go!' She continues, '...you always "go" on green at the traffic lights, don't you Sheena? So, I would imagine, it's all about this hormone working in your body…!' Molly waits for Sheena's reply, then Sheena says, *'Yes, that's right, Molly.'*

Sheena continues, *'Gonadotropins have a main function and that is to work with the gonads, meaning, the gonad is the sex or reproductive gland in both females and males. The female reproductive cell are egg cells, and in males, the reproductive cells are sperm!'* 'Wow!' replies, Caitlin.

Sheena, now has the serotonin hormones sheet in front of her and, says, *'serotonin we all know as the "happy hormone" and that is correct, but like dopamine, sometimes we can have reduced serotonin, when this happens, we can feel sad, unwell, and become sick!'*

She then takes the next image sheet from the pile of papers on the table…!

She says, '…*we have so much more to talk about, but we are running out of time…!*

And I did promise your parents, we would be back by six o'clock on Sunday!'

With so much spoken about, Sheena, then says, *'I think it's time to head back to your homes, however, a new gelato shop has opened in town, and I think it would be a great place to stop, what do you girls think?'* Molly replies, *'how could we resist such an offer…?'*

On the way out of the hospital, Sheena, says to the girls, *'Would you like to meet some of my patients, I have told them that you would both be here at the hospital this afternoon?'*

With such an invitation, both Molly and Caitlin, reply, Caitlin says, *'that would be great, yes, I would love to meet these people.'* Then Molly, says, *'that would be grand, let's do it…!'*

The three make their way to the Children's Ward, where Molly and Caitlin make friends with the girls and boys. When the children see the two girls, they wave or walk to meet them. Caitlin sits on the bed talking to one boy, whose name is John, while Molly walks over to meet a girl called, Sophie. Eventually, all the children gather around Caitlin and John, where they all laugh, tell the story of why they are in hospital, they tell jokes and have fun. Sadly, it was time to leave, both girls promise, *'to come back again!'*

Now, with their visit over and being back home, they both needed to quickly adjust to their swimming schedule and school regime! *'It was very difficult to do',* said Molly to Caitlin on their way to school the following Monday!

Chapter Six
From a girl to a woman

Grandma Shirley was strict about many things, but most of all, she would say, *'When you make a promise to yourself, a positive commitment, to do something, you must always do it, otherwise, you will let yourself down and eventually, you will lose respect for yourself, and who you are, and what you can achieve...!'*

And so, it was with the swimming training schedule that was in place for both Molly and Caitlin!

Not only that, but the girls were also being encouraged to look for little part-time jobs, like dog walking, checking on pets when their owners went on holidays and other little jobs. The payment from these jobs would help them to buy new trainers, or sporting gear, help with buying schoolbooks and other small items that helped their families financially.

Caitlin had her first dog walking job and, on the way, while riding their bikes home from school, on Tuesday, just before their swimming lesson, she told Molly, *'I have my first dog walking job, I will be taking Buster for his walks while Mr and Mrs Fitzpatrick go on holiday; I will start next Saturday afternoon; they are away for two weeks...!'* Molly puffing a bit as they ride over the hill where the bridge goes over the trainline, remarks, *'That's great!'* She then continues, as they ride down the hill, *'I'm going to be looking after Mrs McDermot's rabbits when she goes away next week to see her daughter in Australia; she's gone for six weeks...!'

Molly suddenly stops on her bike, waves Caitlin down, and asks, 'How is Phoebe and the kittens?' Caitlin replies, '...is that why you have stopped, Molly? We'll be late if we don't keep going...!' She again replies to Molly, 'Phoebie and the kittens are fine, Phoebie was sick, and her milk wasn't coming through, now let's keep going...!' With that, they return to cycling and meeting Grandma Shirley at the café!

Grandma Shirley was waiting for the girls; they arrive on time; park their bikes safely at the back of the café, and quickly join, Grandma Shirley, who has her car parked ready, and takes them to the Aquatic Centre!

With Saturday afternoon, Tuesday, and Thursday afternoon, dedicated to swimming, the girls had to now stay focused on their time and how they used it! Grandma Shirley had also organised a coach, who would keep them training, with different targets to meet, during the months ahead!

Grandma Shirley was not only a keen swimmer, when she was younger, she had won many awards in swimming, so she was an extremely dedicated woman once she had her mind set on something!

The coach and Grandma Shirley watched the girls in the pool, with the coach saying to Grandma Shirley, 'there's talent in both girls, but we will need to work *hard with them…! Also, are they prepared to work hard?'*

Well, thought, Grandma Shirley, '…that is something I will need to talk to the girls about…!'

With the swimming over for Tuesday, and in the car, on the way back to the café, Grandma Shirley asks, '…*how far do you girls want to take your swimming?*' Caitlin, first replies to her grandmother, '*well, Grandma Shirley, I've always had a dream of becoming a Paralympian, and if I could train and was good enough to do that, it would be one of my dreams come true!*'

She then asks Molly, '…*and Molly, how about you, would you like to reach an Olympic standard?*' Molly, takes her time to answer Grandma Shirley, then says, '*If I have the ability and talent to do that, I would like to be good enough to go to the Olympics and if the coach thinks I can do this, then I will try my best and work hard…!*'

With the questions answered, the three reach the café, Grandma Shirley puts Caitlin's bike in the back of her car, then they head off for home and the evening meal. By this time, Caitlin was starving and ate every part of the meal she had in front of her, including the Brussel sprouts…!

It was Wednesday and the first class was with Mrs Sheerer. The students had their books open in front of

them and the lesson begun. Mrs Sheerer was very impressed to see how organised her students had become.

Mrs Sheerer announces, *'Tom, would you please give out today's worksheets and the hormone images...?'* Tom, who Caitlin thinks is a nice boy, does exactly as he was asked by the teacher.

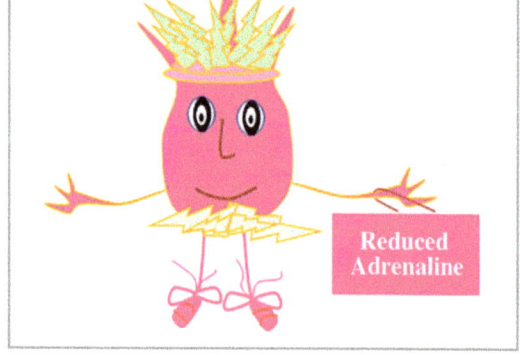

'There are a lot of hormone images to look at and learn about today!' thought Caitlin! With all the images in front of them, the students were ready for their lesson!

Mrs Sheerer begins and has the image of reduced adrenaline on the screen, she says, *'As you become adults, you will have more responsibilities and you need to be aware of how your body works when you feel stressed. When you have upcoming exams, you may feel over-stressed, becoming aware of coping with stress is a message your body sends to your brain saying, "I'm over-stressed, do something about it!" As I have said, many times over, physical exercise is a good way to reduce your 'adrenaline rush', going for a walk, skipping, yoga and other mind-body exercises will help you to reduce too much adrenaline!'*

Caitlin and Molly had seen many of the images when they were with Sheena at the hospital at the weekend, but Molly thought, as she looked at the hormone images, 'It's good to see these images again!' but the pair had not seen the green oxytocin image before!

Mrs Sheerer continues with her lesson and says, 'When we start to learn about hormones and how they work in our body, we can become aware of the feelings or emotions we experience!'

She then continues, 'Our body is made of human and sensitive technology. We are not always aware of the body language our body is sending out in different messages. For instance, when we fall in love, our lips can become redder than is usual! Our body makes these adjustments without any thought about signal from us! Feelings and hormones can be deceptive! We can feel happy and think we are madly in love, when, in fact, it can be infatuation!

When people say or feel 'green with envy', this could be the reversal of the role oxytocin plays in their body, when in fact, they could be jealous or angry with someone and the 'once felt love' turns to anger and frustration. These feelings or reactions may show because of a low release of oxytocin!'

Mrs Sheerer, takes a breath and continues, 'Understanding these hormone differences, is all about growing up and becoming responsible adults. As your body changes, different hormones will start to do their job, females will change differently to males!

The female's brain is different to a male's brain and therefore each person's perception of different events they experience, will be different, and hormones play a big role in individual perception!'

Caitlin, at this point, with her pen, touches Molly, and quietly mumbles, *'We haven't seen all of these hormones before...!'* Molly nods her head in agreement!

Caitlin went back to writing her notes, she then took some time out, looked around her, and then to Molly; her whole class of students were busily working and writing down their notes on what Mrs Sheerer was telling them!

Not a sound could be heard! Mrs Sheerer too, was impressed by what she saw and how good the class was behaving...

With the next slide on the screen, Mrs Sheerer continues, *'the next hormone is melatonin, and many young people may find it difficult to sleep!'*

She stops speaking and asks the group, *'Do any of you find you go to bed tired and though you are tired, once in bed, you cannot sleep?'* With the question asked, many students raise their hands, some want to speak about the difficulty of sleeping, some stay sitting silently in their seat but nod their heads in agreement! Mrs Sheerer can access from the students' reaction, this is a common behaviour and experienced by many young people!

She continues, 'During puberty, many of you will experience restless nights and possibly, not sleep! This is due to how your body is reacting and a possible reduction in melatonin! Science is not sure why this happens at puberty, and more research is ongoing!

Because of this restlessness, many young people play on devices late into the night and early morning. By doing this, the brain becomes over stimulated and if melatonin is low, the chances of having a good night's rest is difficult to achieve!

So, what is the solution? Turn all devices off at least an hour before bed. Go for a walk, play a ball game in the yard or garden, do some deep breathing and relaxation exercises!'

Waiting, Mrs Sheerer, looks at her class as many of the students are still talking about the difficulties of sleeping. She gives the class time, as she understands, 'lack of sleeping' a good night's sleep is more widespread than most parents realise...!'

Mrs Sheerer, now has the next slide on the screen! Caitlin and Molly have seen this slide many times and Mrs Sheerer has spoken about before, Mrs Sheerer wants to remind the students, she says, 'We still have some work to do, and now I want to speak again about dopamine, it is part of your brain's reward system, and helps you to experience pleasure, motivation, love....!'

With the mention of the word 'love' again, some of the students start to talk and laugh, Mrs Sheerer, quickly identifies the students, by saying, *'James and Nathan, it is rude to interrupt me while I'm speaking, please stop and I will continue with the lesson!'* She continues, *'dopamine also helps with how you move, as in physical movement, for instance, when you are playing sport, or when you are concentrating and learning...!'*

She continues, *'By eating a healthy diet full of whole food, you can help with keeping your*

dopamine levels healthy. Foods such as, beef, chicken, almonds, eggs, avocados, and bananas all help you to keep a healthy brain and keeps your dopamine levels balanced!

Having a healthy brain allows you to stay motivated, assists with learning new concepts, allows you to compete at sporting events and generally allows you to feel good which helps you to maintain your overall good health!'

Mrs Sheerer continues, with a change to a serious voice..., 'However, when your dopamine levels are interfered with through vaping, smoking, alcohol consumption, eating too much junk food, drug taking, then you need to think about and recall the messages you are learning in this lesson today...!'

Mrs Sheerer now wants to move on to the next part of the lesson, and says, 'as we all know, there are boys and girls, or males and females, and there is a very good reason for this, it is to allow for survival of the species!

When a female, goes into puberty, her body changes from a girl to a woman...!'

With the introduction of the new part of the lesson, Caitlin knew that it was going to include different areas of how she was growing up; this made her feel a little uncomfortable and could feel herself starting to wriggle in her seat!

Caitlin looked at Molly, she too was doing a little wriggling…! Both Caitlin and Molly had spoken to Jane, Jane had this lesson last year and had given Molly and Caitlin the story on how their bodies would change when they went from a girl to a woman…!

Mrs Sheerer brought the group back into focus and said, *'Before we go to the next part of the lesson, I want to remind you of the slide we learnt about last year…!'*

The image was on the screen, when Mrs Sheerer continues, *'…here we see the stages of the female menstrual cycle!'* Remembering she had a mixed class

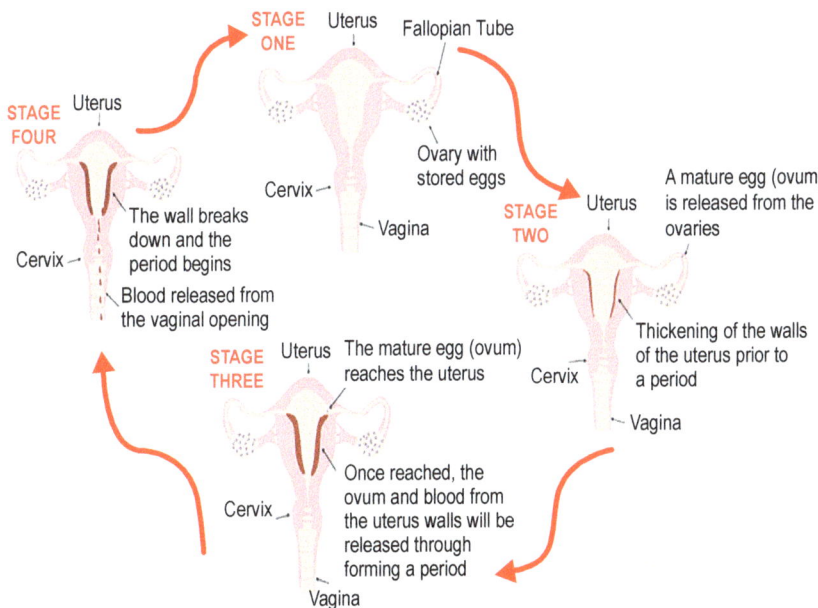

of males and females, and they had seen this slide last

year, she didn't want to linger and take too long on speaking about how the female menstrual cycle worked but knew the importance of the refresher information. She continued, *'I want to remind you of the female menstrual cycle.'* She now has the first stage on the screen and says, *'In this stage the uterus is without the blood lining needed to make a female period!'*

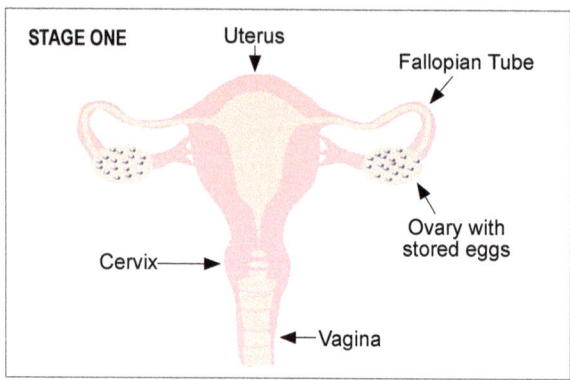

She looks at her students, and asks, *'Are there any questions about Stage One?'* 'Some of the students were busy writing and taking notes, others appeared to be drawing the images...!' She thought!

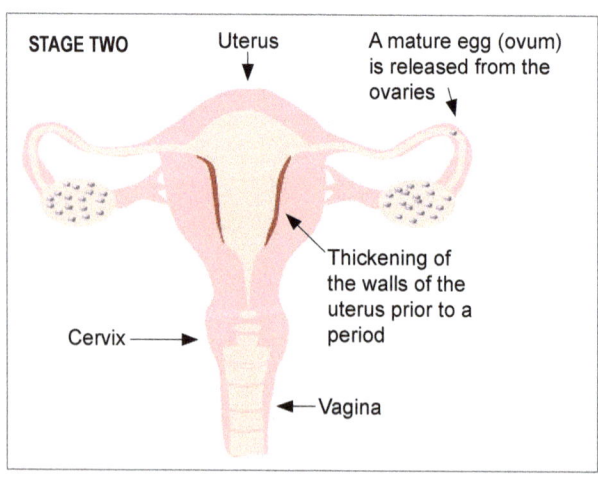

Suddenly, one of the boys who had been busily writing, puts his hand up, and Mrs Sheerer asks, *'You have a question, Max?'* Max replies, *'Does a female go through this every month, Miss?'* *'Thank you, Max,'* she replies, and continues with answering the boy's question, *'Yes, many females go through this every month, some have times when a period does not happen, as in the case of pregnancy, or a stop in a period may be caused through the female experiencing stress or not being well, but most females during their 'child bearing' years have regular monthly periods!'*

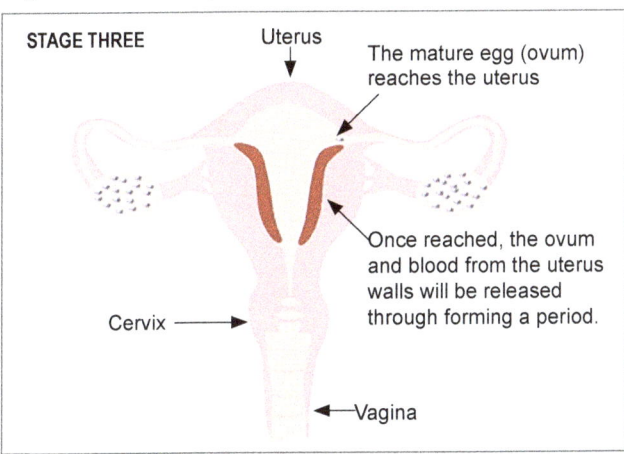

With Max's, question answered, the class go back to taking their notes.

Mrs Sheerer is aware this is a big lesson and wants her students to be well equipped with this vital information, but she is also running out of class time and is keen to push ahead!

The next slide is on the screen, and Mrs Sheerer continues, *'Over the course of twenty-one to thirty-five days; the usual number of days are variable but usually, about twenty- eight, the inner walls of the uterus start to thicken with extra blood, and if the ovum is not fertilised, the female will have a period!'*

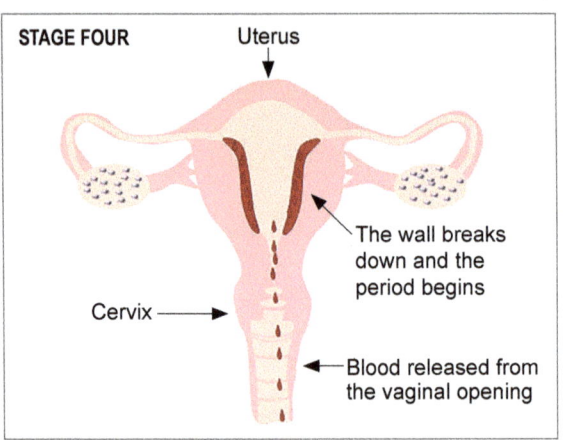

She continues, *'By now, you have all grown and changed, and you know that hormones contribute to many of the changes you are experiencing...!'* She gives the students time to take down notes before she puts the start of her new topic and the images, she is going to show on the screen...!

She continues, *'...human sexuality is about respect for yourself and others. Knowing this subject will enable you to mature, build your confidence and self-esteem and understand the reasons for delaying sexual activity. By taking your time, it will allow you to develop safe, fulfilling, and healthy sexual relationships at the appropriate time throughout life!'*

With her class now back in focus, she wants to concentrate on Stage One, of egg fertilisation.

She now has the new slide on the screen. She says, *'Stage One of fertilisation, the mature female egg leaves the ovary and travels into the fallopian tube, the journey of the egg to the fallopian tube can take from six to twenty-four hours. Once the mature egg is in the fallopian tube, it is referred to as the ovum.*

If fertilisation doesn't take place, the ovum will

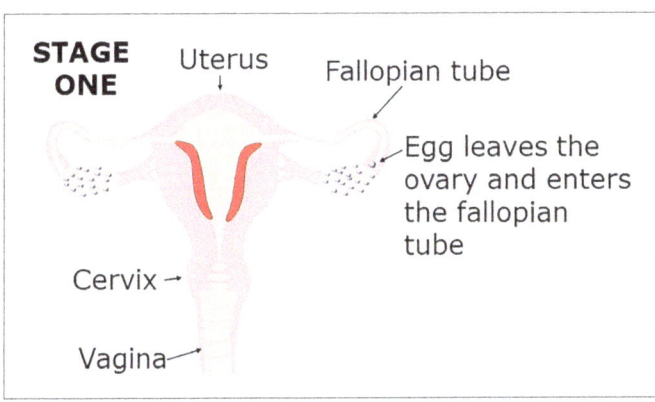

continue its journey until it reaches the uterus and once there, the unfertilised ovum will be released which forms part of the female period, we have seen how this happens on the previous slide...!'

She waits for comments, nothing is said by any student, then continues, *'let's move onto the next slide!'* She notices, many of the girls, and some boys, are taking notes; some are also making sketches of the information they see on the slide! She thinks, '.... this is interesting, with the quietness of the group and work being done, she realises, her students understand the importance of the information!'

Mrs Sheerer continues, *'after sexual intercourse, as can be seen in this next slide, Stage Two, the sperm travels up the female vagina. Students, I want to mention here, sexual intercourse is about two consenting people of the appropriate age, coming together because they want to share each other!'*

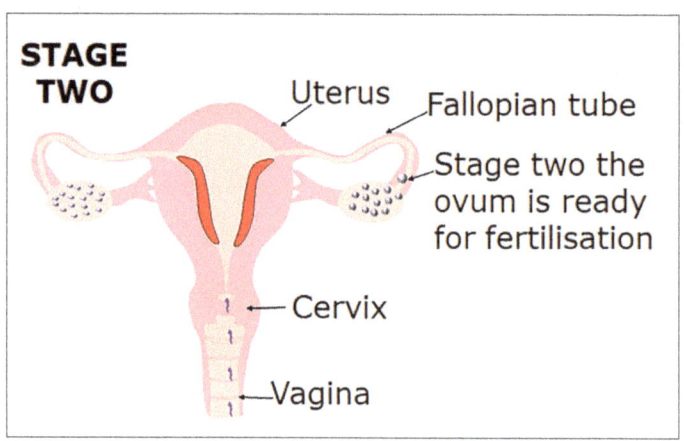

Waiting for the students to look up and ready for the next slide to be seen on the screen, she says, *'In this slide,'* she stops, then continues, *'you can see that sperm are travelling to meet the ovum which is ready for fertilisation...!'* She patiently waits for any student comments, not a sound is heard...!

She continues, '*...it is usually, the healthy sperm that penetrate the female ovum...!'*

She then continues, *'Now, remembering, as I have said a little earlier in the lesson, "...human sexuality is about respect for yourself and others...!"'*

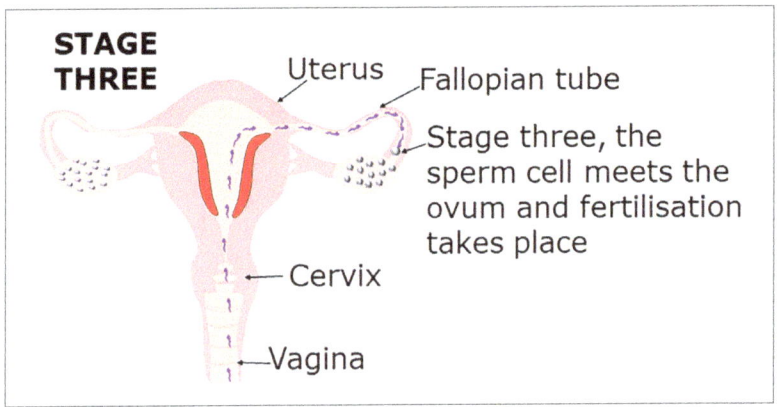

STAGE THREE

Uterus — Fallopian tube

Stage three, the sperm cell meets the ovum and fertilisation takes place

← Cervix

← Vagina

She looks at her students, some are still taking notes, others are studying the slide, one girl is pointing to the slide with her pen, and she is quietly saying, *'cervix, uterus, fallopian tube, and then ovum...hmmm!'* She smiles to herself and then takes down more notes...!

Mrs Sheerer, continues with the lesson saying, *'In Stage Three, the sperm fertilises the ovum. Fertilisation is a complicated process the human body can achieve!'*

Mrs Sheerer continues, *'When ejaculation of sperm from the male body takes place, many millions of sperm are released at one ejaculation!'*

She stops, and asks, *'Are there any questions?'*

She looks at her students, and waits again, and again, asks, *'...are there any questions so far?'*

She then says, '...it is the activation of many of your hormones that takes you on this journey, both into and through puberty and into parenthood...!'

She then says, 'in the next slides, we can see how the fertilised ovum and sperm start to work together! It takes three to four days for a fertilised ovum to reach the uterus!

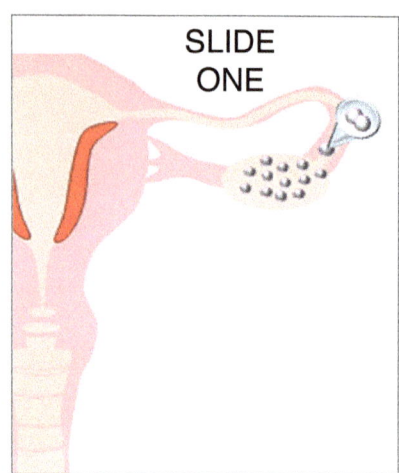

SLIDE ONE

She continues, '...in these slides you can see in the first slide, one cell has divided into two, in the second slide, two cells have divided into four and so the division and multiplying of cells continues!'

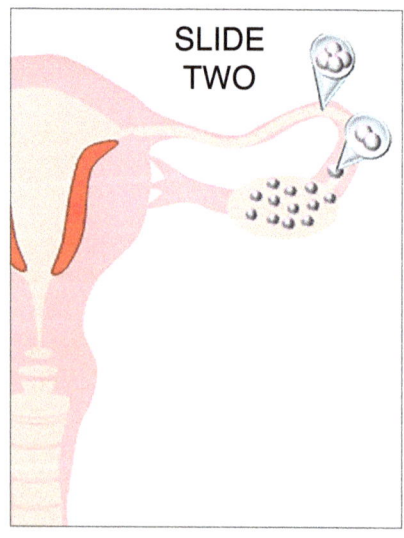

SLIDE TWO

She continues, 'The cells will continue to multiply and divide until the numbers are sufficient to allow them to form a bundle. The number of cells in a bundle is still in discussion by medical researchers!

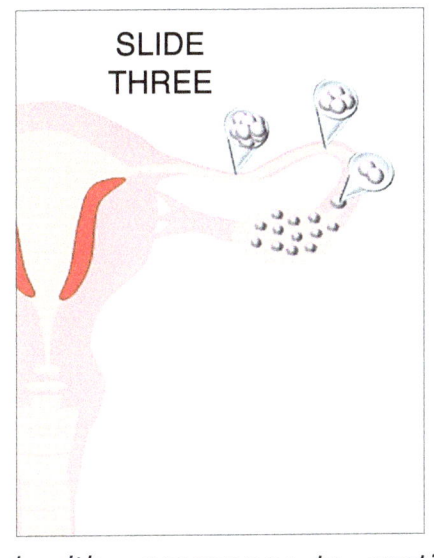

SLIDE THREE

Once the multiplying of cells has taken place, the bundle is ready to move down to the uterus!

In slide three, you can see how the cells are multiplying.' She continues, *'as I have said, this can take several days! We must remember; a bundle may become a baby!'*

She then says, *'for a healthy pregnancy to continue, the fertilised ovum needs to travel and attach itself to the wall of the uterus...!'*

She pauses, then continues, *'An embryo becomes a foetus after eight weeks after conception...! In slide four, you can see how the bundle, has moved, and is attached to the side of the uterus!'* She then says, with a different tone to her voice, *'Some fertilised human cells do not survive!'*

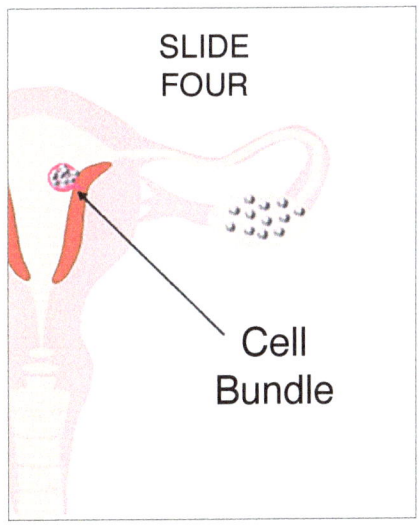

SLIDE FOUR

Cell Bundle

She pauses again, then says to her students, '*A female body is made differently to a male body, and this is with good purpose, it is to create the next generation of people just like yourselves, by doing this, it ensures the future of the species, but...!* She pauses, '*...if in that act of sexual intercourse, respect for each other is lost, it can cause hurt, pain, humiliation, and sadness!*'

With that, the bell rings and it is the end of the lesson.

On the way home and while riding their bikes up the hill that goes over the trainline, Caitlin says to Molly, '*that last lesson with Mrs Sheerer was so interesting, it's made me really think about my body...!*' She takes a moment, then continues as she rides and occasionally looking at Molly, '*I know I have a prosthetic foot, but that is not going to stop me doing anything I want to do in the future!* Molly, looks at her friend, and says, '*what made you think of that?*' Caitlin replied, as they continue to ride, '*I don't know, it's just how I feel!*' With that both the girls carry on riding their bikes until they reach the café!

A few months had passed since Mrs Sheerer had given her talk on puberty. Both girls were working hard within their swimming regime, which delighted Grandma Shirley, and both still had their part-time jobs; they were both saving their money like mad, because the Birmingham Games were *now* only six weeks away!

Part Two
WORKING TOGETHER
For young adults and their family

RESPECT

POINTS FOR TALKING ABOUT

1. Caitlin and Molly have established an adaptable friendship, how does this benefit both girls?
   ....
   ....
   ....
   ....

2. Respect for Grandma Shirley seems to hold the story together. Both Caitlin and Molly listen to what the older lady says, how could you apply this respect in your relationships?
   ....
   ....
   ....
   ....

3. When Sheena comes into the lives of Caitlin and Molly, they respect her knowledge as a doctor and researcher in endocrinology, do you have someone, you could use as a role model like Sheena?
   ....
   ....
   ....
   ....

4. Caitlin has a disability in that she is a paraplegic; she doesn't appear to let anything stop her doing what she wants to do, can you think of a time that you felt 'stopped' and what did you do about it?

……………………………………………………………………………………

……………………………………………………………………………………

……………………………………………………………………………………

……………………………………………………………………………………

5. With her busy life, Caitlin didn't forget about Pheobe the cat and her kittens, she knew that Grandma Shirley would take care of them. However, Molly showed her caring nature as the girls rode their bikes home from school one afternoon; she wanted to know about Phoebe, can you recall a time that either you or a friend cared for a person or animal like Molly did?

……………………………………………………………………………………

……………………………………………………………………………………

……………………………………………………………………………………

……………………………………………………………………………………

……………………………………………………………………………………

……………………………………………………………………………………

…………………………………………………………………………………….

6. Grandma Shirley is an older, wiser lady; she has seen a lot in life, do you have someone you can talk to who is just like Grandma Shirley? Would you like to talk about them?

   ....
   ....
   ....
   ....
   ....

7. Would you say that care, respect, honesty, and trust came through with the story?

   Your answer and discussion:
   ....
   ....
   ....
   ....
   ....
   ....
   ....
   ....
   ....
   ....

8. Caitlin and Molly spend a lot of time together. Because the parents of Caitlin and Molly are so very busy, Grandma Shirley seems to support both the girls in the projects they do. Do you think this is enough or do you think that the girls need to spend more time with their other family members?

   Your answer and or discussion:

   ……………………………………………………………………………
   ……………………………………………………………………………
   ……………………………………………………………………………
   ……………………………………………………………………………
   ……………………………………………………………………………
   ……………………………………………………………………………
   ……………………………………………………………………………
   ……………………………………………………………………………
   ……………………………………………………………………………

YOUR NOTES

Part Three
WORKING TOGETHER
For young adults and their family

OPENING UP THE CONVERSATION

CONTINUING THE JOURNEY

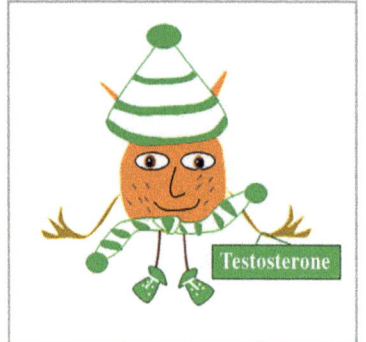

Testosterone is needed for the development of male sex organs. During the mother's pregnancy, testosterone helps in the development of the penis and testes in the unborn child.

During puberty, testosterone, helps the growth of hair in the armpit, around and within the pubic area; it promotes the deepening of the male voice; the development of muscle mass, and strength, and works in the manufacture of sperm production. Other benefits of testosterone; it aids in bone strength and helps to fight bone disorders such as osteoporosis in males and females. Testosterone plays a key role in both males and females.

The hormone Gonadotropin's main function is to help to control the functions within the ovaries and testes. Gonadotropins are important for the regulation and proper functioning related to male and female reproduction.

Gonadotropins are made in the pituitary gland in response to other hormone stimulation in the hypothalamus. The process is carried out by the hypothalamus pituitary gonad axis.

Having an 'adrenaline rush' is great to get you out of danger, but too much adrenaline can make you stressed, and easily upset. In the older male or female, they might turn to smoking, alcohol, gambling, or drug abuse to take a break from the nervous reactions they are experiencing!

Take control of the situation by playing sport, doing relaxation exercises and yoga; all will help to reduce too much adrenaline.

Too much cortisol in your body's system is like too much adrenaline. Take control. If you find you are using destructive substances to keep your nervous reaction in place. STOP, take a breath, and rethink the damage substances can do to your health, behaviour, relationships, and wellbeing.

Remember, you are in charge, not the substances!

The serotonin hormone helps to regulate the brain to normalise certain emotions. It carries messages by transmitting between nerve cells in the brain and to other parts of the body. It is known to regulate mood, digestion, sleep, nausea and breathing. It may act as an anti-depressant through different emotional states or mood swings. Too much serotonin and too little serotonin can lead to different health conditions or outcomes.

Reduced serotonin may be due to a health condition and should be managed by a professional health practitioner. It may lead to depression, anxiety, impulsive behaviour, and sleepless nights.

Oxytocin is known as the 'love hormone', but it has other functions! It is linked to your feelings of empathy, trust, group memories, social bonding, and recognition.

Oxytocin is produced in the hypothalamus, then transported to the pituitary gland at the base of the brain. In females, it helps during childbirth and breastfeeding.

Low oxytocin levels may be related to depression, anxiety, or mood swings. Oxytocin levels can vary depending on life experiences, lifestyle, and the food you eat.

Always seek professional and medical advice if you have concerns.

Melatonin is made in the pineal gland, a small pea-sized gland, found in the middle of the human mid-brain in the brain.

It works as a stimulant to the body and tells us when to sleep or when to wake up!

This hormone works in response to darkness.

The hormone works with your body clock and the forces of night and day. Once evening starts to descend, your body clock kicks in, and you will start to feel sleepy. Melatonin levels, in healthy people are elevated for around twelve hours, allowing people to have a good night's sleep!

Melatonin has many roles, it regulates your sleep cycle; in

females, it plays a role in the menstruation cycle. Research is showing that young people, during puberty, may have low melatonin levels.

In reduced melatonin levels, it may cause mood swings, disruption in sleep pattens and other health conditions.

Like all hormonal levels, each needs to be balanced in your body. By eating a balanced diet that is rich in fruit, vegetables, nuts, and protein, including bananas, berries, cherries, oranges, pineapple, corn, asparagus, tomatoes, olives, broccoli, peanuts, sunflower seeds, flaxseed, and mustard seeds also include in your diet, chicken, eggs, fish, cheese and some whole grain, complex carbohydrate, such as whole grain breads. All these foods help to increase your melatonin level.

Like so many hormones, dopamine is made in your brain. It is important, again, to have the right amount of dopamine, this keeps your thinking and behaviour balanced.

Dopamine has a role in controlling your moods, memory, sleep, concentration, learning and your body movements.

Dopamine helps the nerve cells to send messages to other parts of your brain and in the combination of group cells, it sends messages to the group.

Dopamine is responsible for letting you feel pleasure, motivation, and satisfaction when you achieve something you have been aiming for; the feeling of satisfaction leads to a dopamine rush.

Dopamine is responsible for the delight you experience when you eat nice food. Such delight can be induced by eating unhealthy or junk food, because your brain has registered, through past experiences, the pleasure of eating this food.

Please remember, the taste buds in your mouth are connected to your brain through direct neuron pathways and synapse connections.

Your taste buds are not connected to your stomach! Your stomach will let you know when you are hungry and you need to eat, but your stomach does not tell you what to eat, the quality or goodness of the food! The quality or goodness or lack of goodness in the food you eat, is told to you from your brain!

Having too much dopamine in one part of the brain, or not enough in another part of the brain, can lead to poor impulse control, some aggressive behaviour, binge eating, extreme competitiveness and other addictions.

You can produce too much dopamine in your system by creating bad habits. These habits may include drug taking, alcoholism, gambling, or by creating a craving for an unhealthy diet!

There are many signs that can suggest you have low dopamine levels, some are, continuing to feel sad or lacking in hope and little aspiration and motivation to achieve your goals. You become less excited about happy events in your life. Other signs may be muscle cramps or spasms of stiffness, digestion problems, and a lack of interest in how and why you are going into puberty!

An imbalance of dopamine or other hormones can lead to, stress, inability to sleep, drug abuse, becoming or being obese or eating too much sugar, and saturated fat because of the cravings through a lack of dopamine!

Always remember, a balanced diet of whole food can keep your hormones healthy, and your body and brain balanced.

Continuing the journey – staying in the conversation

It is a good idea to keep the conversation open and fluid with your parents, siblings, or other and appropriate family members when working with this book.

During the story of Caitlin, we spoke a lot about the role hormones play in going from a girl child to a woman! Without hormones working in our body, the female would not mature into womanhood!

We have briefly discussed the female menstrual cycle in this book, having discussed it more deeply in 'Changes' Facing Rosie, from nine-to-eleven-year-old girls. Let's now go back to how the cycle works.

In Stage One, (page 62), it shows a uterus without a period. In Stage Two, the uterus walls are starting to thicken in the early stages of preparing for a period. In Stage Three, the wall of the uterus thickens. In Stage Four, the ovum is not fertilised, this then triggers the thickened wall of blood, in the uterus, to be released allowing a period to happen.

Having gone into some detail of the ovum, you have now become aware of the different stages within the menstrual cycle and at what stage the ovum is ready for fertilisation.

As you continued to read, the teacher of Caitlin and Molly, Mrs Sheerer, took her time to explain how the female egg is fertilised, (page 65).

Once the ovum is fertilised, the period will stop, and the division of fertilised cells takes place.

When cells go from fertilisation to becoming two, then four, then eight, it shows to the young adult the importance of the significant journey the cells make.

The cell bundle continues to multiply while in the fallopian tube. When the cell bundle leaves the fallopian tube, the sack that has developed to protect the cell bundle, attaches to the wall of the uterus; this is now a pregnancy!

The male and female body

It is important for both boys and girls to become familiar with their body; to look and examine their body is a sign of responsibility. When a person knows the intimate parts of their body, they become aware of different changes that can take place in possibly the appearance of lumps, changes in skin colour or other changes that can, and do happen, then medical support can be quickly accessed.

When young people want privacy, it can be with good reason, after all, they are experiencing a lot of changes, not only to their physical body but to the way they think, they are becoming familiar with their brain, they may also start to behave, differently to what we expect!

Again, it is the respect shown for the human body that is paramount with gaining this knowledge.

Many young people start to ask personal questions of themselves, for instance, 'Why am I here?' 'What is my purpose?' all of which are deep, and profound questions to the young adult.

YOUR NOTES

- ✓ RECALL
- ✓ PRODUCTION AND HARVESTING

- ✓ CONSENT
- ✓ FRIENDSHIP
- ✓ COMMUNICATION
- ✓ UNDERSTANDING

YOUR GIRL, BUILDING HER SKILL BASE AND WORKING WITH HER AMAZING BRAIN

Many girls speed ahead with learning in their younger years; they may appear to be smarter than boys, this 'smartness' may be for a short time only, as research is showing, by the time of eighteen, boys do catch up!

As I have previously said, *'the girl's brain is different to the boy's brain...!'* If your girl is showing talent and is smart, nurture this, because there is a lot of competition ahead of her! Nurturing in a quiet, systematic way is a greater benefit to your girl than overt, loud displays that are going to embarrass your daughter.

And bearing in mind, in some world societies, puberty is now starting as low as seven years of age. This can be an embarrassment to many young females. It should not be an embarrassment, it is after all, nature doing what nature does! And, as we know, no human being dictates to nature how to perform! Your daughter is going through 'changes' and it is your responsibility to support her through those changes. Whether you have one, two, three or more girls, the support you offer them is of magical proportion and potential. By understanding, your girl's needs, it is an investment of huge proportion, not only to your daughter, but to the community in which you live. Investing time and effort in our girl at the time of puberty onset is an investment in love and caring for all concerned.

No parent should leave all education to the teachers of our children. We are equally responsible for our children's education. To sit with a child while they learn their words, or learn to read, is an investment of a lifetime, it cannot be transcended by any material gain!

INVOLVEMENT

All children learn in different ways! Some children respond well to action and movement in their learning, others like to see graphics, some like just one-on-one education, for instance, sitting down with a parent at regular times each night to hear her read or pronounce her words, works wonders in forming brain connections. The neurons can go into overdrive when your girl is learning with you sitting by her side. Showing that you care by asking questions that relate to her is also a positive way forward.

Some children have hearing problems, and this is not always detected in a busy class with large numbers of students. If your girl has been suffering with, even mild hearing loss, it will slow her down in her learning capabilities.

I can honestly say, I have never taught a dumb child or a child that cannot learn. All children have a capacity to learn, as I have said, '...*they all learn in different ways...*', and as parents or carers, it is our responsibility to find the technique that allows our girl to learn.

STRUCTURE

The human brain likes order, it does not work well when chaos is surrounding its environment! The brain's architecture and scaffolding, like structure, identity, sameness, and things in their rightful place!

Many children, and some girl's, suffer in their learning if there isn't a structure in place for the learning to be achieved! Each day, your girl's brain is putting down new neuron pathways and synapses that allow learning to take place. If the structure isn't there, your girl may find learning difficult to do. An important part of your girl's learning is to take responsibility for her wellbeing, this includes, from a very early age, possibly as young as five or six, to make their bed in the mornings. How they make their bed doesn't really matter, but the structure and discipline of making the bed allows new neuron pathways to be put down in the child's brain. Other simple jobs can be cleaning out the bird or rabbit cage. If you don't have animals, encourage your girl, at a responsible age, to find small jobs that have payment attached, such as dog walking, looking after other people's pets while they are on holiday, such little tasks help with building life and academic skills.

Age is not a barrier to the simple learning techniques outlined in the above; the sooner you start, the more benefits your child will gain for now and the future.

Do not lose the structure you are putting into place; if there is an interruption, for example, school holidays, travel, sickness or any other reason, the structure must be continued as soon as possible!

RECALL

Please remember, a child's brain, the pre-frontal cortex, is not completely formed until about the age of seven. So, if your girl has memory lapses or doesn't remember something, gently repeat the information. By doing this, you are reinforcing the neuron pathways that were previously put down; you are possibly filling in the blank spaces and then, 'WOW', it makes sense to her!

Even as adults, we work with our long and short-term memories and our children are no different. The one disadvantage they have, is the lack of experience to be able to 'fudge' their way through situations like us older adults!

Remembering, that the child is still putting down neuron pathways in the brain, so the new information they receive daily, is 'NEW' and not old established information that needs to be brought to the surface because of a time lapse, or a convenient dismissal of the information, which as adults, we can do!

PRODUCTION AND HARVESTING

All children have talent and ability, it is inherent in them. It is sad, when a child is considered by others to be a failure, because no child is a failure, they have just learnt in a different way and have not found the way to own their production or how to harvest their ability with the knowledge they've gained at this time in their life!

Even the simplest way of playing can lead to production and harvesting. Learning to cook in the kitchen, showing a girl how to knit, 'one plain, one pearl' can be a great investment in building those much-needed neuron pathways in the brain. Doing anything mechanical, even bringing in the washing before it rains, is a great investment in production and harvesting.

Many 'doing' toys, dolls for girls and carts for boys, go back many thousands of years. Such as the spinning top found in King Tut's tomb that dates back six thousand years ago! And so it is, the more production your girl does, the more and greater neuron pathways are put down inside her brain.

By using:

- ✓ INVOLVEMENT
- ✓ STRUCTURE
- ✓ RECALL
- ✓ PRODUCTION AND HARVESTING

Your girl will move forward in leaps and bounds. Please remember, not one of the steps above can be missed; each has a purpose and reason for being written into this book.

CONTINUING THE JOURNEY

- ✓ CONSENT
- ✓ FRIENDSHIP
- ✓ COMMUNICATION
- ✓ UNDERSTANDING

CONSENT

The age of consent for sexual activity varies, from state to state and from country to country. Having said that, each person's body belongs to no one else but themself; it is not the property of another person and should never be considered in the context of belonging to another!

Your body is your body, and you should never be coerced into giving something of yourself that you don't want to give! Emotional Blackmail is something that is not freely spoken of, but it is a system of abuse that no young male or female should experience. Such comments as:

- ➢ *'If you loved me, you would do this for me...!'*
- ➢ *'Show me you really care and let me do this to you...!'*
- ➢ *'I won't see you again if you don't let me do this...!'*
- ➢ *'If you do this, I will stay with you forever...!'*

And so, the demanding statements are made to another person, all of which should be instantly ignored. If this happens to you, remove yourself from, what has become, a toxic relationship and you don't need this in your life.

In many relationships, there is 'implied' Emotional Blackmail, this is when the words are unspoken and the *assumption* in the relationship assumes the reaction, statement or reply from another person! Such assumptions and answers could be:

> *Assumption, 'Oh, no, they (the second person in the relationship) wouldn't like me to do that...!'*
> *Assumption, 'He/she wouldn't like me to wear that...!'*
> *Assumption, 'She won't mind if you wear her trainers...!'*

The victim in the above becomes powerless and the way forward with this situation is for the victim to voice how they feel, or if that cannot be done, is to move away and out of the coercive relationship.

For many young people learning some of the points above are difficult to do, but the knowledge of knowing how relationships work will give them an experience that will be helpful a little later in life!

FRIENDSHIP

Friendships are very precious to our young males and females. Friendship has three essential ingredients,

- ✓ CARE
- ✓ RESPECT
- ✓ TRUST

If any one of these vital points is lost in a friendship, the friendship usually doesn't survive.

When we CARE for someone, we spend special times together; we remember their birthday or a special day in their life; we let them know that we are thinking of them; we may occasionally buy them a gift because of the bond between us.

When RESPECT is in the relationship, we do not take advantage of our friend, we wait and ask our friend for their opinion, if we can use something of theirs or wait for the right opportunity to ask or speak about sensitive issues.

With TRUST, we know, if we say something to that person, it will not be repeated to other people; we trust that person with our words, precious belongings and more.

Friendship is about reaching out to your friend when you are having a difficult or hard time. You enjoy each other's time and company, you show you think of them by the little things you do for them; friendship has, care, respect and trust built into your relationship.

COMMUNICATION

Communication allows for understanding another person's different emotional needs or wants. Positive communication allows arguments to be settled. Positive communication allows us to interact with our friends and family and to live together. Most people have experienced arguments in the home and how tough it is to live under 'one roof' at these difficult times. Positive communication, (sitting down together and talking things through, allows people to settle their differences and end the argument or dispute).

When we positively communicate, we show we love, care and are happy to be with the people we are with. We may demonstrate this by cooking some biscuits as a surprise, doing the washing up when everybody else has walked away from the dishes in the sink! This doesn't mean you become a 'general dog's body', for everybody else! It means, you talk about the dishes in the sink, and ask, *'Whose turn is it next to do the dishes...?'* Or you might offer to help!

Communication is about giving your time to hear another's story, or to support a friend when they are going through a crisis!

Positive communication allows us to voice our honest opinion and others will give us the time to listen to our side of the story. Positive communication allows us to make changes, positive changes to the world environment where animals and people can be protected.

So, establishing the ground and making ready for positive communication has many benefits in our friendships, relationships with our families and the school and world environments.

UNDERSTANDING

As our girl grows and changes, their level of understanding will also develop into maturity. Understanding that each person has their own set of values, world beliefs and experiences takes time and learning.

We don't all see the same things in the same way. Each person will interpret different words spoken, different experiences and actions taken in different ways. It takes time to develop the 'awareness' needed to understand that we are all different.

YOUR NOTES

Part Five
WORKING TOGETHER
For young adults and their family

HYGEINE AND CARE

YOUR GIRL – HER MATURING BODY AND GROWTH SPURTS

THE BODY DEMANDS

Nature will not be told when puberty can happen to your girl. Your girl's timeclock works with her body's rhythm and will do what it needs to do when the timing is right for her and no one else!

Therefore, many teenagers, if they are not made aware of their body and the changes it will make during puberty, some outcomes can feel overwhelming or intimidating to a young female. Not only is she becoming a young woman, but her body puts other demands on her; she may experience growing pains, especially when she is in bed at night! You may hear a groan or moan coming from her room. Your girl may also start an unexpected period and may not be ready for such an event in her life!

On a serious note, this is not often spoken about; about two years before a girl starts her period, a mucus plug will be released from inside the vagina, this plug is the heralding that her periods are on their way; they still may be eighteen to two years away, but they are coming!

When our children sleep, their body can go into overdrive with growth spurts; it is especially seen with boys, but girls too, can grow and develop while they sleep! When a female starts to develop her breasts, we call this budding. Budding can be a painful experience.

Growth of the breast can and does happen while your daughter sleeps. A small shape seen under a blouse last week, may have grown with a noticeable change the second week!

Not only can our daughters grow at exponential knots, but their body, through hormone interaction, is demanding that change happens; there is no individual choices in what is happening, it will happen regardless! We may look at our growing daughter one day, and find, we silently ask the question, 'Where is my little girl?'

As parents, we must remember, we may see the physical changes taking place, but the young female brain is still growing and will not be mature until your girl is in her mid-twenties! With so many changes happening in her body and brain, there are also the academic and, possibly, the personal skills she is developing! She may also have the thoughts, which may include, *'how will I earn money to survive in the outside world?'*

While many of our girls are safe within their home environment, many may have a long road ahead of them! Many want their freedom, they want to 'stretch their wings' and find out what is on the outside of their comfortable 'home environment?' These yearnings are within many young people, and sometimes, we must, as parents, 'let go', and it can be a difficult and painful process that we too need to do and learn but learn we must!

And while the above is happening, hormones continue to do their job! Understanding that fluctuating hormones may lead to mood swings, tantrums, a painful body while it grows and takes shape, and the development of the monthly menstrual cycle are all part of the puberty journey!

Then there is the development of skin conditions with some young females. Some girls develop a skin condition, known as acne. Acne as a condition is related to the blood vessels in the face and other parts of the body. Acne has also been linked to the rosacea skin condition. The appearance of spots or Acne, on the face, may interfere with your girl's self-esteem and wellbeing. Many teenagers may think that acne is caused through eating too much chocolate or 'junk food', this may contribute to the condition, but it may not be the cause!

Do not use tanning beds, tanning lamps or facial scrubs to reduce the condition, this can and may exaggerate the condition.

1) Twice a day, wash with warm, clean water to remove excess dirt and oil, and
2) Use a sunscreen with a sun protection of 15 or higher!

Acne or rosacea conditions may be linked to simply, becoming aware, 'they are growing up', self-esteem, anxiety, depression, or stress, due to either academic or other 'life demands' they are experiencing.

Other areas of consideration, their body is changing from a child to a woman; this, some young females may feel, is a daunting experience! Give positive encouragement and understanding and commit positive and quality time to talk with your daughter.

Other areas to think about, the body may sweat more than usual, encourage, changing underwear and socks daily, under pants especially, if she loves sport and is a keen sports girl.

Encourage daily showering, including keeping her hair clean. Use a good brand of shampoo, and body wash, possibly without sulphates! These are proving to be harmful to the human skin or body system.

Your girl may experience periods starting during school or while on holiday programs! Before this happens, go with your daughter to the chemist, pharmacy or supermarket and buy a small, but discreet toilet bag that could be used to keep, two sanitary pads, one to two pair of underpants and a deodorant. Suggest putting this into a discreet position in her school bag!

If a period should start at night, and if possible, leave clean sheets where she can have easy access, but also let her know where to put her dirty clothes or bedding.

As a parent, don't be shy, encourage her to start to do her own washing. This is not a punishment but the building of a very valuable life skill that will stay with her throughout her life.

And finally encourage her with dental hygiene keeping her teeth and gums healthy by giving her mouth daily and regular attention with cleaning and brushing her teeth, including gently brushing the tongue to remove any leftover residue from food and drink. Again, these actions are all about building life skills that will stay with her for life.

YOUR NOTES

Part Six
WORKING TOGETHER
For young adults and their family

YOUR GIRL HAS DREAMS

A TIME OF LEARNING AND GROWTH

ADOLESCENCE – A TIME OF ENERGY AND POSITIVE LEARNING – GOING TO THE USA AND ASIA

As a parent, we must be prepared to 'let go' of our girls! We too, can make it difficult on ourselves, if we are not prepared to 'let go!'

She was coming up to sixteen, when she announced, 'I'm going to America as an exchange student, and you can't stop me!' This is the first I knew of her dreams and the idea, that she was becoming her own person!

When my beautiful girl said the above, *'I'm going to America as an exchange student!'* I was devastated. Regardless of how I felt, she went. She too, was now on her life journey. She needed to experience how to grow, cope and manage different situations without her family around her, and within her own natural desires to grow, regardless of the outcome, she needed to go on her own life journey!

For her, the journey was not always easy, she stayed with a family, where there was a clash of personalities with the daughter, a similar age to my daughter, and the situation was no longer manageable!

She was not going to give up. With counselling support from within the country, our girl made her way across the states to Iowa, here she stayed. She continued going to school and learning about American customs, and one year later returned.

Each day a child is away, we as mothers, cannot help but think, 'I wonder what they are doing or up to today?'

The second time away, together with other young people was her trip on a large sailing boat up the coast of Australia, and then on to Vietnam. She was stretching her wings, showing her independence, maturing, and growing into the adult she would eventually become.

Some of the journeys our young people put themselves on, are worrying and concerning for parents, but on their journey, they must go!

YOUR EXTRA NOTES

UNDERSTANDING HOW THE HUMAN BODY GROWS AND MATURES & RELATIONSHIPS

This is a storybook for the young adult, also used as a reader for groups or in classroom settings.

HORMONES WITH HATS
CURRICULUM OBJECTIVES – UNITED KINGDOM (UK)

Natural body changes for girls between School Years 7 to 9, ages 11-14 years.

(Health and Wellbeing, Relationships, and Living in the Wider World) Relationships Education, Relationships and Sex Education (RSE) and Health Education.

'Effective RSE does not encourage early sexual experimentation. It should teach young people to understand human sexuality and to respect themselves and others. It enables young people to mature, build their confidence and self-esteem and understand the reasons for delaying sexual activity. Effective RSE also supports people, throughout life, to develop safe, fulfilling, and healthy sexual relationships, at the appropriate time.' [2]

CURRICULUM OBJECTIVES – AUSTRALIA

Incorporating and supporting Year 7-9, ages 11-14 years. Personal, Social and Community Health (ACPPS070 – ACPPS076 – ACPPS071 – ACPPS072 – ACPPS073 – and other related areas of the Curriculum including: TLF-IDM021182 Scootle.edu.au).

---

[2] Relationships and Sex Education (RSE) (Secondary) - GOV.UK (www.gov.uk) Extracted from 'statutory guidance Relationships Education, Relationships and Sex Education (RSE) and Health Education & Australia: https://www.scootle.edu.au

ONLINE SCHOOL PACKAGES

Full Potential Training offers a range of education packages. With our school packages for 'CHANGES', Children Growing Up, we cover the sensitive area of puberty and the changes that naturally occur in males and females. The story book at the beginning of each book allows the child to become familiar with the role that hormones play in making these body changes happen.

For young females with the ages of eleven to fourteen, we have developed, 'CHANGES' Facing Jai. The girls' book is 'Changes' Facing Caitlin. The books have been developed with discretion and to allow the child to quietly absorb the story board about the changes they are either going through or about to go through. We cover many sensitive areas of the subject of puberty, and how the female and male body works as the change occurs.

We offer a complete online package, which includes the story book. The online education packages do include the changes that both males and females go through during the time of puberty. They are not directed to one sex but both males and females. Once ordered, the package is downloaded from our server to the school, college, or holiday programme at your location.

The Package for Changes, Females and Males, Children between the ages of 11-14 has four by one-hour sessions, including a continuous 'voice over' with each slide. There are pause times for discussion and some question-and-answer sequences.

We ask that courses be ordered at least two (2) months in advance, this allows us to print and deliver the children's books to your location and in time for the lessons.

The packages meet (please see page 112), both the Australian and United Kingdom objectives within Social Community Health and Relationship and Sex Education.

For more information, please email,

        admin@fullpotentialtraining.com.au

    Or, see our website, www.fullpotentialtraining.com.au

FAMILY PACKAGES

For many people, discussing puberty and the 'Changes' that take place within the human body are private discussions. They may not be easy discussions to have, but it is a necessary part of a parent's responsibility to their child or children.

For those people, we have developed Family Packages that include one book and a CD that is the same as the School Package.

If this allows you to discuss this topic with your family in private, please contact, admin@fullpotentialtraining.com.au

www.ingramcontent.com/pod-product-compliance
Lightning Source LLC
Chambersburg PA
CBHW062038290426
44109CB00026B/2660